Canada Law Book Topics in Dispute Resolution

Dispute Resolution in the Insurance Industry

Canadian Cataloguing in Publication Data

Grant, Anne E. (Anne Elizabeth), 1958-
    Dispute resolution in the insurance industry: a practical guide

Includes bibliographical references and index.
ISBN 0-88804-346-5

1. Insurance law – Canada. 2. Dispute resolution (Law) – Canada.
I. Title.

KE1149.G72 2000   346.71'086   C00-932312-0
KF1164.G72 2000

This book is dedicated
to the memory of
my mother, Margaret,
my greatest critic
and most devoted supporter

Canada Law Book Topics in Dispute Resolution

This series is intended to provide lawyers with general insight into what the various methods of dispute resolution mean for their particular area of practice. Others, such as professionals in dispute resolution, will benefit from an understanding of how their practice affects lawyers.

While various forms of mediation and arbitration have long been part of the legal system, in recent years the search for alternatives to expensive and overly prolonged litigation has taken on more urgency. Individuals and organizations see a way to avoid the often punishing costs of litigation. Business people can expect swift resolution of their disputes. Governments, responsible for court systems which seem overburdened by ever-increasing case loads, see a way to restore an efficient, cost-effective justice system. One can see this in the establishment in Ontario of a mandatory mediation program, which is still in its infancy. Everyone stands to benefit from a way of solving disputes which is largely free from the "win/lose" nature of the traditional adversarial legal system. By now "alternative dispute resolution" ("ADR") has become a permanent feature of the legal landscape.

Lawyers increasingly encounter ADR in one of its several forms. Some wish themselves to become practitioners of "alternative" or "appropriate" dispute resolution. But the various forms of ADR require a very different state of mind, a different attitude towards resolving disputes between parties. Attitudes that worked well during traditional litigation are not appropriate during mediation. These books will make this clear.

Each of these books sets out how dispute resolution works in the context of one particular practice area of law. We contemplate volumes on all the major practice areas, including family law, insurance law, employment law, and corporate and commercial law.

The books set out the roles of lawyers, as well as professional mediators and clients, in the dispute resolution process. They provide general definitions of terms and situations which occur. They also provide an orientation to specific legal issues and to the special ethical and professional issues which typically arise in one specialized area of law.

All of the authors are highly visible and well-regarded authorities in their area of practice. As the series grows, it will make a significant contribution to the growing literature on this increasingly important aspect of the Canadian legal system.

CANADA LAW BOOK INC.

Foreword

The use of dispute resolution as an alternative and as an adjunct to traditional litigation processes has become commonplace in the insurance sector. Responsible advocates assess and strategically utilize the appropriate process for their case. The use of alternative dispute resolution processes has grown beyond negotiation, mediation and arbitration to encompass preventative planning measures such as the use of ADR clauses in policies and contracts. Major administrative tribunals such as the Insurance Corporation of British Columbia and the Financial Services Commission of Ontario have institutionalized the use of mediation and arbitration for motor vehicle disputes. In Ontario, Rule 24.1 of the *Rules of Civil Procedure*, R.R.O. 1990, Reg. 194, mandates the use of mediation in the early stages of civil proceedings.

Increasingly, ADR is being used as part of ad hoc dispute resolution systems designed to deal with special classes of claimants. A decision of the Ontario courts handed down in October 2000 illustrates this point. In *Williams v. Mutual Life Assurance Co. of Canada* (unreported, October 18, 2000, Ont. S.C.J., court file nos. 96-CU-111307 and 97-CU-127295), a case involving the issue of "premium offset" (or "vanishing premium"), Cumming J. dismissed a motion to certify a class action suit and commented on the use of an ADR program set up to assist claimants. In his reasons, the judge recognized that the insurer's ADR program used arm's length third parties, professional arbitrators and timely disclosure of relevant documents, and it provided for procedural fairness and transparency.

As a result of this growing trend involving the use of dispute resolution systems, insurance professionals must appreciate the various ADR choices available. To be prepared, insurance professionals require a straightforward, insurance-specific text offering practitioners guidance regarding the appropriate process to select and how to strategically represent their clients' interests in whichever dispute resolution forum is chosen.

Dispute Resolution in the Insurance Industry: A Practical Guide is such a resource. Anne Grant's extensive experience as a mediator of insurance disputes in both mandated and private forums is shared with the reader through her many practical examples and tips. Grant's experience as a dispute resolution consultant in the insurance context is evident in her description of the design of an in-house screening tool as well as her observations regarding the design and implementation of an ad hoc dispute resolution process for handling special classes of claimants.

Consistent with the realities of resolving disputes in the 21st century, Grant provides insurance professionals with a how-to guide containing checklists, case studies and summaries of key points. The indexing, language and format of her text make the topics easy to locate and read.

I have had the pleasure of working with Anne Grant as a fellow student in the first offering of the Masters-of-Law in ADR at Osgoode Hall Law School and as a fellow member of the executive of the ADR section, Canadian Bar Association – Ontario. As a dispute resolution consultant and mediator with extensive exposure to the use of DR in insurance disputes, I am pleased to recommend *Dispute Resolution in the Insurance Industry: A Practical Guide* as an essential and timely addition to the Canada Law Book Topics in Dispute Resolution series, and to any insurance professional's or advocate's library.

Elana H. Fleischmann, LL.B, LL.M (ADR)
Co-ordinator and Legal Counsel
Dispute Resolution Office
Ministry of the Attorney General (Ontario)
November 10, 2000

Preface

The writing of this book has been a stimulating and challenging endeavour! While the continually changing and evolving landscape of dispute resolution in Canada was at times a challenge, I realized that the principles governing excellence in advocacy remain the same. In other words, in order to support, represent and further their clients' cause, advocates need to understand process choices, and they need to recognize their own strengths and weaknesses as well as those of their counterparts.

To compile this book, I drew on my experience as a former advocate in the negotiation, mediation and arbitration context and on my current experience as an intervenor in the insurance context. I also reviewed the literature already available in the field. What has resulted is an intensely practical guide which strives to provide insight and information about the strategic choices for ADR advocates in the insurance industry.

A work such as this is not only the result of the author's efforts, but it is also a product of those around her. I would like to extend a very warm "thank you" to Elana Fleischmann, counsel at the Dispute Resolution Office of the Ontario Ministry of the Attorney General, for her encouragement and insights. Her experiences in both the public and private context were invaluable. Those at Canada Law Book should also be thanked for encouraging me in my vision. In particular, I would like to thank my editor, Howard Davidson, for his encouragement throughout the publishing process. Tremendous thanks to Stuart Mutch, counsel at Manulife Canada (formerly a mediator at the Ontario Financial Services Commission), and to R. Gail Goodman of Heenan Blaikie, formerly of Aetna Life Insurance of Canada, for their assistance in reviewing the manuscript. My gratitude also goes out to my partners Judi Clarkson and Alan Alexandroff at Mediated Solutions Incorporated. Their knowledge, humour, support and insights were critical to the completion of this manuscript. A very special thanks also to Cerys McLellan for her unstinting good nature, hours beyond the call of duty, and tremendous administrative support in ensuring the timely submission of this manuscript.

My love and thanks go out also to my husband John and our daughters Alexandra and Elizabeth who gave me the time and the space to write.

Anne E. Grant
MEDIATED SOLUTIONS INCORPORATED
Toronto, Ontario

Table of Contents

xi

Part B: ADR Core Concepts and Skills

Part C: Other ADR Applications

Introduction

This book emerged from an identified need on the part of practising advocates in the insurance context for a set of clear, concise explanations of the principles of alternative dispute resolution (ADR). The practice of ADR has become commonplace and institutionalized in the insurance sector. Consequently, effective advocates require not only a basic understanding of the theory and concepts behind it, but also direction with regard to strategic choices regarding any given ADR process.

This book is for all advocates in the insurance industry including such insurance professionals as claims adjusters, adjudicators and lawyers, as well as administrative professionals working in the insurance sector. Advocacy in ADR has moved beyond the basics into an increasingly sophisticated approach to dispute resolution. With this reality in mind, this book is divided into three sections:

Part A: ADR Prerequisites

Part B: ADR Core Concepts and Skills

Part C: Other ADR Applications.

Each chapter begins with a bulleted list of key concepts summarizing the "need to know" aspects of ADR contained within that chapter. Throughout the book, an attempt has been made to provide both a primer with regard to the ADR concepts being discussed as well as a "beyond basics" section setting out a more sophisticated approach for the advanced practitioner. Each chapter concludes with practical checklists, lists of ADR organizations, and/or legislation relevant to the topic of the chapter.

PART A: ADR PREREQUISITES

Part A of the book examines ADR definitions and methods for distinguishing between different ADR options. Chapter 1 reviews commonly held definitions of dispute resolution processes along the ADR spectrum. It includes extensive discussion on how to pre-screen insurance files for suitability for one of the four main types of ADR: direct negotiation, mediation, early neutral evaluation or arbitration. In addition to examining the choices which advocates make regarding the selection of a particular ADR process, Chapter 1 explores the various considerations to be reviewed prior to selecting a suitable ADR practitioner.

Chapter 2 sets out the advocate's role and responsibilities in preparing a case, the client and an ADR brief. This chapter also examines in detail the advocate's strategic preparation for the ADR session.

PART B: ADR CORE CONCEPTS AND SKILLS

Part B of the book focuses on the three most common ADR processes: negotiation, mediation and arbitration. Chapter 3 reviews common negotiation theories and models used in the insurance context. The typical stages of the negotiation process are described, and there is a discussion of positional/competitive negotiation versus co-operative/interest-based negotiation. In this chapter, advocates are encouraged to examine their own negotiation style, identify the styles and preferences of their negotiation counterpart, and consider the attributes of both effective aggressive negotiators and effective co-operative negotiators.

Chapter 4 describes the models of mediation commonly used in the insurance context. In this chapter, the reader is given the opportunity to analyze the mediation steps involved in two hypothetical insurance cases. These steps include negotiation, use of a mediator, generating options and ultimately reaching an agreement. At the conclusion of the chapter, there are checklists for advocates to consider when preparing their mediation files, as well as examples of agreements to mediate. Given the increasing use of mandated mediation in the courts and tribunals, this chapter also sets out questions for advocates to consider in these institutionalized ADR settings.

Chapter 5 reviews the arbitration process from the perspective of the beginning practitioner. In a privately arranged arbitration process, the advance negotiation of a detailed agreement to arbitrate is of fundamental importance. An arbitration agreement typically sets out the jurisdiction of the arbitrator, rules regarding disclosure, rules of evidence and the powers of the arbitrator to make orders. A comprehensive arbitration agreement is included and discussed in this chapter.

PART C: OTHER ADR APPLICATIONS

Part C of the book refers to other ADR applications in the insurance industry. Specifically, Chapter 6 discusses the drafting of dispute resolution clauses in the insurance context, and Chapter 7 reviews the considerations involved in designing ADR processes. In Chapter 7, the author explores a step-by-step design exercise for a generic in-house ADR and case management system and the design of a hypothetical ad hoc process for special classes of claimants. The use of ADR in both of these areas is becoming increasingly prevalent in the insurance context.

Finally, the book ends with a conclusion summarizing the key lessons for an ADR advocate in the insurance industry. Read on and learn!

Part A

ADR Prerequisites

ADR Choices

⎛ **Key Concepts** ⎞

- ADR refers to a series of dispute resolution processes ranging from collaborative, consensual processes such as negotiation and mediation to adjudicative processes including arbitration and litigation.
- The most common ADR processes used in the insurance industry are negotiation, mediation, neutral evaluation and arbitration.
- Understanding ADR options is fundamental to strategic selection of a process and effective preparation.
- Advocates distinguish among ADR choices by considering the party's desire to control the process or outcome, the party's need for confidentiality, and the role and purpose of any third party intervenor.
- When choosing an ADR process, effective advocates consider the spectrum of ADR options, the substance of the case including the issues in dispute, cost factors, the relationships between the parties, and the stage of the lawsuit/dispute.
- Effective ADR advocates use screening criteria to systematically select an ADR process. Such criteria may include: cost-benefit analysis, consideration of legal risks, the precedent value of the file, and the availability of supporting documentation.
- When choosing a third party intervenor, strategic ADR advocates consider training, qualifications, experience, degree of process and substantive expertise, and practical considerations such as ability to travel, cost and scheduling.
- Agreements to mediate or arbitrate should clearly outline the terms of intervention, any cost and payment arrangements, the identity of the parties, the

name of the mediator, the date and time of the mediation session(s), and the
issues to be mediated.

1. ADR CHOICES – INTRODUCTION

This chapter highlights the basic definitions of the ADR processes commonly
used in the insurance context. Topics discussed include a review of the different
approaches to ADR process selection as well as the selection of an appropriate
ADR practitioner.

2. TYPES OF ADR INTERVENTIONS

In the insurance sector, the most common types of ADR interventions are
negotiation, mediation, neutral evaluation and arbitration. These processes can be
compared by examining:

(a) the extent to which each process is confidential;
(b) whether a third party neutral is used; and
(c) the role of the third party intervenor.

ADR process options can also be evaluated by examining the level of input the
parties have in choosing the intervenor, managing the process and controlling any
outcomes.

Negotiation has been described as the situation where two or more parties,
either directly or through representatives, enter into discussions among themselves with the intention of resolving issues in dispute absent the assistance of an
outside party. Negotiation is a confidential process. The parties directly control
the terms of the process as well as the outcome. Different models of negotiation
are discussed in Chapter 3.

Mediation involves a structured process whereby an external third party
neutral – the mediator – assists two or more parties to resolve their dispute on
their own terms. The mediator may recommend ways to resolve the dispute but
has no power to decide for the parties or to bind them to any particular solution.
In a privately contracted mediation, the parties choose the intervenor, determine
the intervenor's role, decide the terms of the mediation, and retain control over
the outcome. In mediation mandated by legislation or regulation, the choice of
intervenor may be limited or non-existent. It is important to note that even in a
mandatory mediation regime such as the Ontario Mandatory Mediation Program
under Rule 24.1 of the *Rules of Civil Procedure*,[1] or a mediation before the
Financial Services Commission of Ontario[2] or the Insurance Commission of
British Columbia, the process is confidential. In addition, the parties retain control

---

[1] R.R.O. 1990, Reg. 194.
[2] The Financial Services Commission is merging with the Ontario Securities Commission. The
    name of the merged organization was not known at the time of writing this book. The merger
    is expected to take effect in March 2001.

over whether they settle or not. Models of mediation commonly used in the insurance context are discussed in Chapter 4.

Neutral evaluation is a process whereby an accepted substantive or technical expert – the neutral evaluator – evaluates the relative strengths and weaknesses of the positions advanced by the parties. Based on this assessment, the third party forms an opinion as to the probable outcome at adjudication and advises the parties accordingly. Neutral evaluation is not binding. It is informative only. In a private neutral evaluation, the parties choose their own substantive expert and control the mandate or terms of that expert's intervention. Neutral evaluation can also form part of a mediator's role. In either case, the parties retain control over the outcome of the case. In some institutionalized settings such as pre-trial or pre-hearing conferences, the presiding neutral may offer an evaluation of the legal merits of the file.

Arbitration is the process whereby an impartial third party neutral – the arbitrator – hears and assesses the opposing sides of a dispute and makes a decision as to how the dispute will be resolved. This decision may be advisory only, or it may bind the disputing parties. Commonly, arbitration is an evidence-based process within a set of mutually agreed to or prescribed rules of procedure. Arbitration has been described as a type of private litigation. Both arbitration and litigation are evidence-based. In both processes, a trier of fact hears argument from each party and makes a decision about the issues. This can result in a binding outcome for the parties. In both processes, the parties use a structured format to present facts and argument within known rules of procedure. In arbitration, the rules of procedure may be determined or modified on consent by the parties. The parties can also determine the identity, skill or training of the trier of fact. In mandated arbitration at an administrative tribunal such as the Financial Services Commission of Ontario, however, the parties have little or no control over the identity of the arbitrator or the rules of procedure. Arbitration advocacy, terms and conditions are discussed in Chapter 5.

(a) Comparison of ADR Process Options to Litigation

The table that follows summarizes the similarities and differences between traditional litigation and the four ADR process choices described on pp. 8-9.

COMPARISON OF ADR PROCESS OPTIONS

Type of Process	Use of Third Party	Selection of Neutral Third Party	Role of Third Party	Control of Terms of Process	Control of Outcome	Confidentiality
Negotiation	No	N/A	N/A	Parties control	Parties control	Yes
Mediation	Yes	Sometimes parties select	Facilitates exploration of mutual options for resolution	Parties control	Parties control	Yes
Neutral Evaluation	Yes	Sometimes parties select	Provides non-binding evaluation of merits of case	Parties may control	Non-binding assessment of case	Yes
Arbitration	Yes	Sometimes parties select	Renders evidence-based decision in accordance with agreed procedure	Parties control	Arbitration imposes outcome	Perhaps
Litigation	Yes	Parties do not select	Intervenor is an evidence-based decision-maker in accordance with publicly accepted rules of procedure	Parties do not control	Court or tribunal imposes decision	No

(b) Selecting the Best Process

The benefits of ADR include the promotion of early, cost-effective and mutually agreeable dispute resolution. A critical step for the ADR advocate is to assess the case and determine the appropriate ADR process and what third party dispute resolver is required. Advocates need to consider whether a consensus-based process such as negotiation or mediation is desirable, or whether a binding adjudication such as arbitration or litigation is indicated. Neutral evaluation may be a tool to assist the parties in coming to a consensus-based settlement.

Evaluating a case for ADR is a matter of judgment. It cannot be reduced to a statistical formula favouring any particular process. Some legal counsel and insurance companies have developed screening tools to ensure systematic selection of cases and referral to ADR. Advocates should consider the following screening criteria, which are listed in a checklist in Appendix 1.1 at the end of this chapter.

Type of issue: In insurance litigation, the issues can be extremely varied and broad. They may include:

(a) allegations of professional negligence;
(b) contractual disputes over the interpretation of policy terms;
(c) quantum amounts for damages incurred in property disputes;
(d) breach of contract disputes;
(e) other kinds of insured claims; and
(f) disputes between insurance companies in the case of subrogated claims.

Consideration should be given to the type of dispute and the history that the individual lawyer or organization has had in negotiating, mediating or sending such disputes to neutral evaluation or to arbitration.

Identity of any group insurer: For many institutional defendants, the presence of a group policy is a significant business interest which may need to be considered or preserved. For example, the denial of a large number of long-term disability claims in one major institution caused the client to cease using the insurer for its employee benefits packages. The client's decision arose from a perception of "high maintenance" in handling employee and union complaints about the policy.

Percentage of the claim that is reinsured: A large number of insurance files are reinsured. While the reinsurer may not play a direct role in handling disputes or providing authority to settle, the presence of a reinsurer can be a factor in deciding whether to go to a private, consensus-based process such as negotiation or mediation. As previously stated, in these processes, timing and outcome are within the control of the parties as opposed to submitting a file to the rigours of a trial.

Evidence/presence of fraudulent activity: In assessing the utility of negotiating, mediating or sending a case to neutral evaluation or arbitration, consideration must be given to the evidence which has been gathered to date. An indication of fraudulent activity such as negative surveillance results may influence an institutional defendant to send the file to an early mediation in order to ensure that the plaintiff is aware of the case against him or her. In another case, such evidence may motivate a party to pursue the case in court in order to expose activities it feels are reprehensible.

Presence or absence of supporting documentation: It is clear in insurance files that the presence of supporting documentation such as proof of income loss, receipts for treatment, medical records, expert reports and other objective documentation are influential in determining whether an institutional client will consider settling a case or not. It is well known that insurance companies require objective data or documentary evidence before any kind of significant settlement discussions can occur. When direct negotiations have failed for this reason, mediation can be a way of ensuring that the required documentation is provided in a timely fashion. Many advocates have made exchange of relevant documentation a prerequisite to mediation and have set time limits for production. In this way, all parties can make an informed decision about negotiating a settlement.

Quantum in issue: The relative size of the quantum in issue is a very influential factor. Files with a large amount of money at issue may be ideal to send to mediation or an early process in order to reduce long-term liability. At the same time, a plaintiff that is out of pocket for defined amounts of money may desire an opportunity to expeditiously resolve the case without the delays associated with litigation. The quantum in issue can be a very subjective consideration for some advocates and should be considered in conjunction with the other procedural and substantive needs of the parties. Some advocates may find that the quantum is so small that it makes sense to try to resolve the case earlier rather than later.

Cost-benefit analysis: It is becoming a more common practice for both defence and plaintiff counsel to maintain a running tab of the administrative and legal costs of a particular file. In many institutional cases, the organization may actually do a projection of the anticipated costs, which may include the time spent by in-house staff working on the file, client time on the file, and the time of legal clerks and internal and external counsel. Insurance companies may conduct an analysis of the relationship between reserves and the actual and anticipated costs of pursuing a file. In some cases, a file may already be identified as costing more than the average for similar files.

Length of time the file has been open: A further consideration for both defence and plaintiff counsel is the length of time the file has been open. The economic costs of maintaining an active file over months and years is tangible and can be measured. Costs include administrative time, fees for legal counsel, and the costs of the time of both the plaintiff and the defendant. Institutional clients may have business reasons for moving files through efficiently, just as plaintiffs may experience frustration from excessive periods between activities on the file. Concerns about the economic and psychological costs of delay are often cited as reasons for using alternative means of dispute resolution.

Litigation analysis: Potential liabilities at trial are always part of the risk analysis to determine whether to use direct negotiation, mediation or some evaluative method such as neutral evaluation or arbitration. Typically, legal risk assessment is done by counsel.

Stage of the lawsuit: For some lawyers and clients, there is a preferred entry point for various types of ADR. In the insurance industry, it is becoming more common to have mediations conducted prior to the issuance of a statement of claim. The next most common entry point for private mediation is post-discovery, when the respective counsel feel they have collected sufficient relevant information to conduct a proper litigation analysis of the file. Court-mandated ADR may force the parties to mediation in a short time-frame post filing the statement of defence. If a file is case-managed and likely to be referred to mandatory mediation, this may preclude suggesting neutral evaluation or arbitration. Many files are referred to mediation at a later date, such as at pre-trial or after the trial has commenced, particularly where it has been determined that the parties would benefit from exploring settlement options.

Jurisdiction of the case: ADR practices and statutory requirements may differ in various jurisdictions. Many insurance counsel, both for the plaintiff and the defence, have recognized that there are different approaches to mediation at various entry points in the different provinces and territories of Canada. In some provinces, the choices of ADR are limited, and the local Bar has less experience with the various ADR options. This may influence whether a case is sent to ADR or not.

Identified trends: Many advocates who work on insurance files have had professional relationships with particular insurers or with specific plaintiffs or plaintiff counsel. The history of this relationship may inform the decision of whether to pursue ADR. For example, one insurance company identified a particular plaintiff counsel in a certain geographical location with whom it was extremely difficult to deal. The identified counsel took extreme positions and had developed a reputation for not bargaining in good faith. In that situation, the institutional insurer made it known among their counsel that if that lawyer was on a plaintiff's file, the insurer would not consent to voluntary mediation and would only participate in mediation if mandated to do so by a court.

Precedent value of the file: In some cases, the parties may require a public legal precedent to clarify a policy, set a benchmark for future claims, or rationalize the expenditure of money on a particular area by an organization. When a precedent is required, the choice of mediation may not be the preferred process, given the confidentiality associated with any settlement arrived at in the mediation process.

Public scrutiny: In some high profile cases, both plaintiff and defence Bar may choose the confidential private method of direct negotiation, mediation or arbitration to avoid the adverse effects of media attention to their clients. For example, in the case of a train derailment, it may be in the best interests of the institutional client to settle quickly and privately through the mediation process rather than submitting to a series of public court cases. In a situation where the client is a prominent, publicly accountable organization, there may be utility in opting for a private and confidential means of exploring settlement.

Relationship aspect of the dispute: The relationship between the insurer and a group of insured individuals may be pivotal in deciding whether to utilize ADR. In the case of subrogated claims, where both the plaintiff and the defendant are institutional insurers, there may be professional and corporate relationship issues which promote the use of negotiation or mediation to settle differences expeditiously and in a business-like manner. The number of mergers of insurance companies in recent years has resulted in many insurers considering ADR to avoid potential conflicts of interest.

Need for coercion: In some cases, there has been a lack of sharing of relevant information and pertinent documents. The scheduling of a mediation with particular prerequisites can persuade parties to share information at an earlier stage.

(c) Exceptions to Choosing a Consensus-Based ADR Process

The use of consensus-based ADR processes is a strategic choice. Advocates should carefully consider whether negotiation or mediation is appropriate in the following cases:[3]

* **When fraud is alleged:** A basic prerequisite for effective negotiation and mediation is trust. Allegations of fraud are often accompanied by concerns over the honesty and credibility of the parties.

* **When a precedent or a declaratory judgment is required:** Individual and organizational interests may include the need for a public award or precedent and a declaratory judgment to enforce any structured settlement.

* **When the parties are not willing to settle:** A difficult situation arises when one or more the parties are not willing to have constructive discussions about resolution. The old adage "You can lead a horse to water" applies to ADR process choices.

* **When the damages are not yet quantifiable:** In a case where the damages have not yet been quantified, the use of ADR may be premature. Advocates should distinguish between cases where damages cannot be quantified and those where the level or extent of damage is not yet fully understood. For example, in a case where the plaintiff is a minor, the full impact of the alleged injuries may not be quantified until the child is grown. On the other hand, in a case where the damage to the long-term goodwill of a business is unknown, a consensus-based discussion, with or without an intervenor, may be beneficial to finding some common ground.

---

[3] T.M. Sourdin and J. David Scott, *Court-Connected Mediation, National Best Practice Guidelines* (Centre for Dispute Resolution, University of Technology, Sydney, and the Centre for Court Policy and Administration of Wollongong, in association with the Law Council of Australia, 1994).

(d) Using ADR to Overcome Barriers to Settlement

Authors Stephen B. Goldberg and Frank E.A. Sanders, in their influential article "Fitting the Forum to the Fuss: A User Friendly Guide to Selecting an ADR Procedure",[4] suggest that the barriers to settlement be analyzed as an indicator in selecting the appropriate ADR process for a particular set of circumstances. They identify 10 common barriers to resolution which should be considered in choosing an ADR process. These are listed in a checklist in Appendix 1.2 of this chapter. A discussion of them follows.

Poor communication: In the insurance context, where the parties do not typically have long-term personal contact, the relationship between the parties and/or their lawyers may be so dysfunctional that the parties cannot effectively communicate. Lack of trust may preclude meaningful discussion and negate even constructive negotiation proposals. Successful negotiation is predicated on an ability to communicate clearly and effectively. Further, different communication styles, approaches and methods may prevent the parties from understanding and appreciating each other's needs and concerns. In a situation where poor communication is a barrier to settlement, direct negotiation does not always solve the roadblock. Mediation can be a useful process since the third party neutral facilitates and directs the communication between the parties. The mediator can refocus the parties on a discussion of the factors leading to the dispute and can separate the parties physically if necessary. A mediator's facilitative role can assist in smoothing over inappropriate statements and assisting the parties in effectively listening to each other. Likewise, the mediator's role as referee or enforcer of ground rules can assist in dealing with inappropriate or dysfunctional behaviour.

Need to express emotion: The parties may have a need to express their anger or other emotions to each other. For example, the plaintiff may be very angry with his or her insurer for having denied a claim. Emotions may also surface with regard to the party's representatives and legal counsel. In one situation, settlement discussions were disrupted because litigation counsel were so angry with each other that they could not speak courteously. When venting is necessary, the mediation process is the best choice. The mediator provides an informal atmosphere which encourages full participation by both the disputants and their lawyers. The mediator acts as a witness who controls the venting process and ensures that the parties are able to safely express their views. Through active listening, the mediator may be able to reframe explosive statements to acknowledge the emotion but at the same time prevent loss of face by the other party. Goldberg and Sanders suggest that while some venting is possible in evaluative ADR processes such as neutral evaluation and arbitration, those processes are less conducive to the expression of feelings.

Different views of the facts: When the parties disagree as to the facts of the case, settlement discussions are very difficult. A skilled mediator can persuade

---

[4]   *The Negotiation Journal*, Vol. 10, No. 1, January 1994.

the parties to put aside their factual dispute while at the same time agreeing on a mutually acceptable resolution. If, however, determination of the disputed facts is essential to resolution of the case, then some form of adjudication may be required. This could include arbitration and possibly adjudication in a formal court setting. Goldberg and Sanders suggest that neutral evaluation can also aid in overcoming conflicting evaluations of the facts by providing a neutral assessment of the case.

Different views of the legal outcome if a settlement is not reached: In many insurance files, the disputants agree on the facts but disagree on the legal interpretation of those facts. The plaintiff may assert that, on the basis of the agreed facts, he or she has a 70% likelihood of success, while the defendant, with equal confidence, may assert that he or she has the same chance of success. In mediation, the intervenor can often persuade the parties to resolve their dispute without necessarily determining which of their positions is correct. If a settlement cannot be reached through constructive discussion, a non-binding assessment by an experienced neutral can be helpful in bringing about a resolution.

Issues of principle: In some disputes, one or both of the parties may be attached to a fundamental principle which may need to be compromised or "parked" if the parties are to resolve their dispute. For example, in a professional negligence file, the plaintiff may feel strongly that the professional caused harm and that he or she must be punished in order to effect revenge. Another example is where an institutional client feels strongly that it will not pay "one red cent" to a slip and fall victim because the incident occurred on a public street in a Canadian winter. Such principles and values often create a high amount of intensity so that evaluative techniques may not be helpful in reaching a settlement. In the mediation process, the intervenor may be able to find a creative way of reconciling the seemingly conflicting values of the disputants by assisting the parties to look at compromises which satisfy other interests. In the example where the injured party feels that the professional should be punished, the characterization of the resolution may satisfy that need. There may be additional interests in ensuring that the same thing does not happen to someone else. This need or concern can be addressed in a resolution. In the case where the defendant's representative feels strongly that the public should be responsible for their own accidents in public places, addressing ways of preventing such accidents from happening in the future may be helpful in arriving at a mutually acceptable resolution.

Constituency pressures: When one of the parties represents an institution or group, agreement may be impeded or influenced by pressures from the constituent members. For example, an institutional insurer may have organizational interests in settling a file before year-end, while the advocate or negotiator may have staked his or her reputation on obtaining a certain result. In the insurance industry, the representatives at the table very often represent a large corporate interest with needs and objectives which they do not necessarily wish to share with the insured plaintiff. This becomes particularly difficult when there are multiple defendants representing various institutions. A mediator can assist in such situations by conducting pre-meeting conferences with the defendants to try to come up with options to address divergent concerns. A mediator can also solve the problem of a negotiator's investment in a particular solution by serving as a sounding board or scapegoat. This allows the representative to blame an unsatisfactory outcome on pressure exerted by the mediator. Other non-binding processes such as neutral evaluation can serve a similar function. Goldberg and Sanders state that evaluation by a neutral can demonstrate to one or more of the constituent groups that its position is unlikely to prevail and hence the settlement proposed by its representative is reasonable.

Linkage to other disputes: In situations where the resolution of one dispute has an effect on other disputes involving one or more of the same parties, such linking can complicate negotiations and lead to an impasse. A good example is the individual resolution of a series of claims by similarly situated claimants. The same lawyer may represent one or more of a specified group of claimants without necessarily invoking the complexity of a class action lawsuit. In such a case, the institutional defendants may have some difficulty in discussing settlement because of the settlement's potential impact on other files. The practical result is a hidden agenda and the challenge of being influenced by individuals who are not at the table and are not necessarily direct players. In this scenario, mediation can be useful by providing a forum to devise a settlement formula which meets the institutional needs as well as the needs of the individual plaintiffs. The issue of linkage can also be addressed in other non-binding processes such as neutral evaluation. However, ideally the neutral should be in a position to play a mediation role as well as an evaluative role.

Multiple parties: Situations involving multiple parties with divergent interests raise similar problems to those raised under the headings of diverse constituencies and issue linkages. Goldberg and Sanders advise that in the case of multiple parties, a mediation will sometimes succeed in finding a balance of interests which satisfies all involved. It should be noted that a skilled mediator will propose flexible processes to ensure that parties with like interests can meet expeditiously.

Different lawyer-client interests: It is a fact of life that lawyers and clients may have divergent attitudes and interests concerning resolution. Goldberg and Sanders suggest that this may be a matter of personality or economics. A lawyer who is paid on an hourly basis may be less interested in settlement than a lawyer who is paid on a contingent fee basis. Goldberg and Sanders submit that this potential conflict of interest should promote settlement processes which provide for direct involvement by the client.

Jackpot syndrome: In many insurance files, one barrier to settlement is the plaintiff's operational view that conducting a trial is akin to winning the lottery. If the plaintiff believes that a large amount of money for punitive damages is likely, this may preclude positive discussions directly in negotiation or in the presence of a mediator. To overcome this barrier, the parties often require some kind of evaluation, either through a neutral evaluation or in the form of an arbitration award.

Goldberg and Sanders recommend that a "rule of presumptive mediation" is the best policy in pre-screening cases. In their article, they observe that mediation has the greatest likelihood of overcoming all the previously described impediments with the exception of different views of the facts and law and the jackpot syndrome. In any event, a skilled mediator can often facilitate resolution without the necessity of obtaining agreement on the disputed questions of law or facts. Under this approach, the mediator first attempts to resolve the dispute by using customary mediation techniques within a prescribed time frame. By obtaining a clear sense of the parties' goals, the mediator can then make an informed process recommendation and direct the parties to neutral evaluation, arbitration and/or back to trial.

(e) Strategic Considerations for Using Mediation

Although the most common reason for using mediation is to resolve the case, effective advocates consider the mediation process for achieving other goals. Trial advocates have identified the following as rationale for selecting the mediation process.[5] A checklist of these considerations is provided in Appendix 1.3.

Resolve part, if not all, of the case: Effective ADR advocates give consideration to settling a portion of their case even if the entire case cannot be resolved. The author has conducted mediations where agreement was reached on the amount of damages, but the parties chose to proceed with litigation with regard to liability. In another example, the parties agreed on liability, but went before a judge to determine damages.

Narrow or focus the issues: Statements of claim commonly include every possible avenue of recovery. Pursuing all avenues without considering what is provable or realistic wastes the parties' time and may not elicit sympathy from a judge. Mediation is an opportunity to narrow and realistically focus the issues after the advocates have gained a more comprehensive understanding of the facts in dispute.

Test a theory of the claim or defence: The practice of law is an art, not a science, and most advocates recognize the gray areas in any legal argument. Some advocates use the evaluative form of mediation to obtain a neutral opinion regarding their theory of the claim or defence. This can also be achieved through the use of early neutral evaluation or the non-binding view of a judge or adjudicator during a pre-hearing or pre-trial conference.

Evaluate the case through discovery: Effective advocates continually evaluate their case on the basis of the facts and the credibility of the witnesses and the evidence. The full completion of discovery in a complex case can be costly and risky. Some advocates utilize mediation pre- or mid-discovery to inform themselves as to whether to continue with the discovery or to modify their line of questioning. Issues have been raised about the ethics and good faith of using

---

[5] John W. Cooley, *Mediation Advocacy* (Notre Dame, Indiana: National Institute for Trial Advocacy, 1996), available for order at www.nita.org/bookorder.asp.

mediation in this way. However, as all participants in mediation have equal access to each other's clients and theory of the case, as well as an equal opportunity to re-evaluate their own case, the negative effects are minimal.

See how the opposing party would impress the jury as a witness: The effective advocate is fully aware that persuasion is a large aspect of advocacy. Persuasion is achieved through effective speaking, positive demeanour and non-verbal cues such as appearance and presentation. The persuasive potential of any witness is an important factor to be considered in assessing one's case. Mediation is an ideal opportunity to view the other client in a "without prejudice" format. However, it also allows the mediation counterpart to view one's own client in a similar light.

Get an independent assessment of one's client as a convincing witness: Effective advocates assess their own clients continually as part of conducting the file. However, it may be informative to observe the client with the opposing party in a non-prejudicial format such as mediation. For example, in a professional negligence claim, the author is aware of a situation where the defendant professional presented as confident and articulate in the private meetings with the insurance counsel, but turned into a mass of nerves when confronted by the plaintiff. The counsel in that case reported that it was advantageous to have this information prior to a trial situation and stated that it was an important consideration in settling the case.

Obtain early discovery in a small case in order to facilitate early settlement: Most advocates do a cost/benefit analysis to determine whether a case should be conducted through prolonged, expensive litigation or settled as quickly as possible. Where the quantum is likely to be smaller than the costs of running the trial, advocates should consider using mediation to ensure a mutual understanding of the facts as well as an opportunity to pursue settlement discussions.

Work out a procedural schedule in a complex case: The author is aware of a number of situations where advocates used the mediation session to negotiate a mutually agreed litigation schedule or to expedite the discovery process. Where there are multiple parties and counsel, the logistics of scheduling alone can be a nightmare. Mediation can be an opportunity to discuss and agree on procedural steps with the assistance of a neutral chairperson.

Resolve discovery disputes: American attorney and author John W. Cooley[6] states that mediation is often used to settle discovery differences quickly as opposed to resorting to motions to compel, or to protect some types of documents from, disclosure.

Use a mediator to communicate creative proposals: In the adversarial world of litigation, some advocates find it difficult to propose creative solutions outside the scope of traditional litigation remedies. This may be due to concerns about diluting one's professional reputation as a litigator or anticipation that the opposing party will not be open to ideas from an adversary. Use of a mediator gives

---

[6] *Supra.*

both parties an opportunity to maintain their professional litigation stance because ownership of the idea is diverted to the mediator. This allows both parties to save face in accepting or rejecting such a proposal.

Use a mediator to disclose favourable "bombshell" information: Building on the rationale discussed under the previous heading, the mediator can also assist in communicating information detrimental to one party's case. The classic example is disclosure of damaging surveillance evidence. The use of surveillance and other demonstrative evidence in the mediation process is discussed on pp. 89-90. Some litigators persist in the notion that this information should be held back and used in a type of "trial by ambush" manoeuvre before a judge and jury. Other advocates consider that their clients may have business and/or economic interest in settling the file without the cost of a trial. These advocates use mediation as a safe forum to disclose difficult evidence or facts in an attempt to persuade rather than threaten the opposing party into settling. The author is aware of one insurance file where the insurance company had evidence that the plaintiff had falsified documents. With the assistance of the mediator, this fact was communicated and proved to plaintiff's counsel without unnecessary hysterics and denials. As a result, plaintiff counsel obtained written direction from his client to withdraw the case, and the insurance company paid the out-of-pocket disbursements of plaintiff counsel in recognition of his professionalism and co-operation.

Use a mediator to filter and diffuse harmful information: Just as the effective advocate uses the mediation process to share influential facts or information with the other side, the advocate may use the mediator to diffuse facts harmful to his or her own case.

Determine possible trade-offs in a multi-party case: The dynamics of litigation sometimes preclude ascertaining the true interests of the parties. By meeting privately with the parties, a mediator can explore the case and assist the parties to prioritize their desired settlement options and canvass possible opportunities for joint gain.

Determine common interests between the parties: Where there are multiple plaintiffs or defendants, inevitably there is some limit on the amount or types of damages which can be recovered. In one motor vehicle accident tort claim, settlement of the wrongful death portion of the claim was limited by lack of information regarding the final quantum of damages for the injured passengers in the other vehicle. Since the amount of money available under the policy was limited and both claims were likely to add up to the full amount, the first plaintiff and defendant had a joint interest in ascertaining the quantum of the second plaintiff. As a result of mediation, they identified this mutual limitation and worked together to create an expedited process to evaluate the second plaintiff's claim. In another file, multiple defendants met to discuss how they could jointly address the claim of a single plaintiff. A mediator assisted the defendant in identifying how to allocate any damages and communicating settlement offers on behalf of the entire group of defendants.

3. LITIGATION VERSUS ARBITRATION

Advocates who come to the conclusion that consensus-based ADR such as negotiation or mediation is not appropriate for their situation should consider the following in making a determination as to whether to pursue private arbitration or litigation in the courts:[7]

1. Does the party need to secure a decision in a public setting?
2. Does the party want to risk the spectre of a massive or unpredictable jury award?
3. Is establishment of precedent or articulation of public policy an important goal for either party?
4. Does either party seek public vindication of its reputation, position or claim?
5. Is a vital corporate interest involved which requires the full range of procedural protection afforded by a court in full appeal rights?
6. Is there a need for continuing court supervision of the case or the parties?
7. Does the delay associated with litigation significantly assist one party?
8. Is the law on a determinative legal issue well settled in favour of one party, allowing for effective use of summary judgment or some other dispositive motion?
9. Does one party prefer to retain appeal rights?
10. Is the case linked to other pending claims of significance to either party?
11. Does the case require an understanding of complex or technical factual issues?
12. Given what is at stake, are the transition costs of pursuing litigation small when compared to what either side can realistically expect to recover or save?

FEATURES OF LITIGATION VERSUS ARBITRATION[8]

Litigation	Arbitration
Public process	Private process
Any party can institute	Parties must agree to use
Adversarial procedure	May be less adversarial
Formal, inflexible	Less formal, more flexible

---

[7] CPR Institute for Dispute Resolution, "Questions to Assess Litigation versus Arbitration", http://www.cpradr.org. Further information which can be gleamed from this website includes "Thirty Questions to Assess ADR Suitability Regarding Consensual ADR". To access these articles, click on "Procedures & Clauses" on the CPR home page, then on "ADR Suitability Screen" on the next page.

[8] CPR Institute for Dispute Resolution, "Features of Litigation versus Arbitration", http://www.cpradr.org. Click on "Procedures & Clauses" on the CPR home page, then on "ADR Suitability Screen" on the next page.

Litigation	Arbitration
Statutory rules of procedure govern	Simpler rules of procedure; evidence rules usually not strictly applied; parties may agree to modify
Broad discovery	Discovery typically limited to documentation production; interrogatories or depositions permitted depending on selected rules of procedure
Adjudicators are generalist judge/jury	Arbitrators may be party-selected experts
Adjudicators apply the law; their decision sets precedents	Arbitrators apply party-selected standards (law, business standards or equity); failure to apply is generally not reversible error; decisions do not set precedents
Broad right of appeal	Grounds to void award limited to arbitrator's fraud, bias and the like
Remedies can include compensatory and punitive damages and injunctive relief	Arbitrators can grant compensatory damages and injunctive relief; preliminary injunctive relief may be difficult to obtain on an emergency basis; parties can limit arbitrator's authority to award certain damages
High transaction costs	Can reduce costs
Delay (docket)	Usually reduces delay to commencement of hearing; hearings may be intermittent depending on selected procedure and arbitrator's schedule

4. WHAT STEPS SHOULD ADVOCATES CONSIDER TO EFFECTIVELY IMPLEMENT ADR IN THEIR PRACTICE?[9]

Systematically select files and process: Approaches to the selection of files for various types of ADR can be done through the pre-selection of categories of cases or through tailored, customized selection for each individual file. Institutions have used ADR screening tools and contract clauses to assist the parties in determining which files should go to what type of ADR process. Selection of files to send to ADR has been done at the discretion of the institutional client (*e.g.*, adjusters) and/or legal counsel or by team review, and has also been contracted out to external consultants. Some organizations conduct periodic reviews of cases to determine ADR potential and to fine-tune in-house screening processes. Both individual and institutional advocates use lists of preferred ADR providers to save time in identifying acceptable intervenors for particular files. The use of in-house case management systems is discussed more fully in Chapter 7.

---

[9] See also the checklist in Appendix 1.4.

Obtain consent from the parties: Prior to convening a case for any type of ADR such as mediation, neutral evaluation or arbitration, it is useful to elicit consent in principle from all the parties. It is presupposed that mandatory mediation referral will be convened in accordance with the procedures prescribed by the mandating authority. However, in the case of private ADR, all parties must agree. It is useful to talk about the benefits and risks with one's client to ensure understanding of the nature of the proposed ADR process.

Make a written offer to go to ADR: One technique which has been successfully used by many advocates, particularly where there is no pre-existing relationship between the parties and/or their legal counsel, is to make the offer to go to mediation or arbitration in writing. This ensures that all parties are clear about what process is being proposed and about any terms and conditions, and it ensures that the suggestion will be communicated to the client.

Propose a limited number of suitable intervenors: Sometimes the parties do not agree to the first intervenor who is proposed. Therefore, it is useful to propose several in order to expedite the convening process. Advocates should encourage opposing counsel to counter-propose acceptable intervenors if they cannot agree in the first instance.

Consider terms and conditions: Part of the convening process is determining exactly how the selected ADR process will proceed. Some advocates and their clients may elect to offer to pay costs and/or may obtain an estimate from the intervenor to assist in planning for any type of ADR process.

Consider who will convene the selected ADR process: Convening an ADR process is extremely time-consuming, yet many institutional clients utilize their legal counsel for this purpose. To address cost and efficiency issues, some organizations designate an administrative person to fulfill the convening role and/or they contract this role out to a dispute resolution firm specifically for the purpose of screening and setting up mediation or arbitration.

Verify ADR arrangements in writing: It is useful when convening cases for ADR to build on existing relationships between the parties and to be open to each party's needs and concerns with regard to process and substance. Once an agreed-to process, intervenor and date have been selected, either the intervenor or the parties should verify these arrangements in writing to ensure mutual understanding and to avoid confusion.

Contract with a dispute resolver: Professional dispute resolution practitioners use formal written agreements to mediate and/or arbitrate. These agreements will be discussed in detail in Chapters 4 and 5 respectively. Examples of private mediation and arbitration agreements are included at the end of those chapters.

5. CONSIDERATIONS IN CHOOSING A THIRD PARTY INTERVENOR

In the case of insurance files, it generally falls to counsel to select a third party intervenor. Some institutional clients have designated in-house personnel who select intervenors and convene mediation and other forms of ADR. The following eight areas should be considered in choosing a third party intervenor:

(1) dispute resolution professional orientation and style
(2) training, qualifications and expertise
(3) process and/or substantive expertise
(4) curriculum vitae and references
(5) location, price and scheduling
(6) personal experience and observations
(7) interview of the intervenor
(8) professional directories and rosters

Dispute resolution orientation and style: As discussed in Chapters 3 to 5, there are different models and approaches to negotiation, mediation and arbitration. Different intervenors will have different preferences and styles in their approach to ADR. This should be considered by those selecting a third party intervenor in order to ensure maximum utilization of the process. For example, some mediators may use an evaluative approach, preferring to assess the merits of the case and give the parties a non-binding indication of their opinion of the file. In other cases, the parties may be more interested in a mediator who facilitates constructive discussion and helps the parties to examine underlying interests, needs and concerns. A good mediator should be able to utilize different tools to meet the process needs of the parties. ADR advocates should inquire as to a particular professional's ADR approach and style as part of the selection process.

Training, qualifications and experience: The practice of mediation in North America is not regulated at the present time. As a result, mediators have various levels of training. It is useful to examine the background of a proposed intervenor to ensure that he or she has completed a minimum 40-hour intensive mediation program. Most full-time mediators or dispute resolution practitioners have completed many hundreds of hours of education and have training on how to handle difficult parties and multiple parties, as well as techniques to move parties past impasse. Qualifications should be considered in conjunction with ADR experience. In selecting a third party intervenor, it is useful to ask the intervenor how many mediations, neutral evaluations and/or arbitrations he or she has conducted and in what context.

Process or substantive expertise: Some parties prefer that the third party intervenor be a substantive expert in the particular area of the dispute. For example, many insurance professionals have become successful mediators in the insurance field. Parties should consider whether they require a process professional with extended expertise in order to keep the parties talking and move them past impasse, or whether they want a substantive expert who can switch roles and provide a neutral evaluation in the context of mediation. In the case of a written arbitration award, the parties may wish to know how much background the arbitrator has in the substantive area of the dispute.

Curriculum vitae and references: Those selecting a third party intervenor should review the professional summary of any proposed intervenor and consider speaking to that person's references. This due diligence is helpful in differentiating between similarly qualified dispute resolution professionals and making a selection in the context of a specific file or where a specific approach is required.

Location, price and scheduling: Another consideration in choosing a third party intervenor is geographical location. If the file is to be mediated in Saskatoon, for example, are the parties willing to pay the travel expenses for a mediator to come from Vancouver? The fees for mediators and arbitrators can vary substantially. It is acceptable to ask a potential third party intervenor to provide an estimate as to length of time needed for preparation and mediation and what is expected in the way of disbursements and cancellation fees. Scheduling can also be a difficult issue in selecting a third party intervenor and obtaining dates which accommodate all the parties. If the goal of setting up a mediation or an arbitration is to expedite the proceedings, a dispute resolution professional who is setting dates a year ahead would not be helpful.

Personal experience and observations: In the field of ADR, personal experience and word of mouth are extremely important. It is useful to speak to colleagues and ask what their experience has been over time, as well as applying personal knowledge of dispute resolution professionals' techniques and expertise. One note of caution should be observed. When discussing the experiences colleagues have had with various dispute resolution professionals, consideration should be given to whether they have had extensive or limited experience with ADR. For example, an individual who has been to one mediation which did not settle may blame the mediator for not settling the file and may give a negative reference. Those who have had experiences with various types of dispute resolution professionals in the insurance context may be better able to comment knowledgeably about any given professional's ability to handle different kinds of situations.

Interview of the intervenor: One practice which is common in the insurance field is picking up the phone and calling the intervenor directly. The previous items of consideration can form a basis for this one-on-one discussion. In the case of complex files where there are multiple parties or a staged process may be required, clients have been known to interview the intervenor in advance in order to assess which in a group of potential intervenors would be most appropriate. This is commonly used by the government in the case of multiple claims.

Professional directories and rosters: There are resources to assist in identifying qualified, experienced individuals. These include professional associations such as the Arbitration and Mediation Institute of Canada Inc. and its various professional affiliates, and the Canadian Bar Association. A list of Canadian ADR organizations is included in Appendix 1.6 of this chapter. Many mediation programs such as court-annexed programs and other programs administered by the government use any agreed-to roster of mediators who have met prescribed requirements. These rosters can be a good starting point for obtaining the names of suitable intervenors for various types of ADR. Some organizations will even match clients geographically and substantively. For example, if a client requires an intervenor with some health care background and process expertise in northern Ontario, one of these organizations may be able to assist in finding a mediator in that district with those qualifications.

APPENDIX 1.1
CHECKLIST OF POSSIBLE ADR SCREENING CRITERIA[10]

- ☐ type of issue
- ☐ identity of group insurer
- ☐ identity of the other parties and their relationships
- ☐ percentage of the claim which is to be reinsured
- ☐ evidence or presence of fraudulent activity
- ☐ presence or absence of supporting documentation
- ☐ quantum in issue
- ☐ cost-benefit analysis
  - ☐ current administrative and legal costs of the file
  - ☐ anticipated administrative and legal costs of the file
  - ☐ presence of reserves in relation to the actual and anticipated costs of pursuing the file
  - ☐ total cost of the file in relation to average costs: has the file been identified as over the limit?
  - ☐ length of time the file has been open
- ☐ litigation analysis
  - ☐ stage of the lawsuit
  - ☐ pre-pleadings
  - ☐ case-managed
  - ☐ court-mandated ADR
  - ☐ pre-discovery
  - ☐ post-discovery
  - ☐ pre-trial
  - ☐ trial preparation
  - ☐ trial commenced
- ☐ province/jurisdiction of the case
- ☐ identified trends
- ☐ counsel on file

---

[10] For a discussion of these points, see pp. 11-14.

☐ precedent value of the file
☐ public scrutiny
☐ relationship aspect of the dispute
☐ need for coercion

APPENDIX 1.2
TEN COMMON BARRIERS TO RESOLVING CASES
(GOLDBERG AND SANDERS)[11]

☐ poor communication
☐ need to express emotion
☐ different views of the facts
☐ different views of the law
☐ important principles
☐ constituency pressures
☐ linkage to other disputes
☐ multiple parties
☐ different lawyer-client interests
☐ jackpot syndrome

APPENDIX 1.3
STRATEGIC CONSIDERATIONS FOR USING MEDIATION[12]

☐ Resolve part, if not all of the case.
☐ Narrow or focus the issues.
☐ Test a theory of the claim or defence.
☐ Evaluate the case through discovery.
☐ See how the opposing party would impress the jury as a witness.
☐ Get an independent assessment of one's client as a convincing witness.
☐ Obtain early discovery in a small case in order to facilitate early settlement.
☐ Work out a procedural schedule in a complex case.
☐ Resolve discovery disputes.
☐ Use a mediator to communicate creative proposals.
☐ Use a mediator to disclose favourable "bombshell" information.
☐ Use a mediator to filter and diffuse harmful information.
☐ Determine possible trade-offs in a multi-party case.
☐ Determine common interests between the parties.

---

[11] For a discussion of these points, see pp. 15-18.
[12] For a discussion of these points, see pp. 18-20.

APPENDIX 1.4
STEPS AN ADVOCATE SHOULD CONSIDER IN IMPLEMENTING AN ADR PROCESS[13]

☐ Systematically select files and process.

☐ Obtain the consent of the parties.

☐ Make a written offer to go to ADR.

☐ Propose a limited number of suitable intervenors.

☐ Consider terms and conditions.

☐ Consider who will convene the selected ADR process.

☐ Verify ADR arrangements in writing.

☐ Contract with a dispute resolver.

APPENDIX 1.5
CONSIDERATIONS IN CHOOSING A THIRD PARTY INTERVENOR[14]

☐ dispute resolution orientation and style

☐ training, qualifications and expertise

☐ process and/or substantive expert

☐ review of curriculum vitae and references

☐ location, price and scheduling

☐ personal experience and observations

☐ interview of the intervenor

☐ professional directories and rosters

APPENDIX 1.6
ADR ORGANIZATIONS

Alternative Dispute Resolution: National Section
Canadian Bar Association
50 O'Connor Street, Suite 905
Ottawa, Ontario K1P 6L2   Tel.: 1-800-267-8860

Alternative Dispute Resolution Section
Canadian Bar Association – Ontario
20 Toronto Street, Suite 200
Toronto, Ontario M5C 2B8   Tel.: (416) 369-1047

American Arbitration Association
140 West 51st Street
New York, N.Y. 10020-1203, U.S.A.   Tel.: (212) 484-4000

---

[13] For a discussion of these points, see pp. 22-3.
[14] For a discussion of these points, see pp. 23-6.

Arbitration and Mediation Institute of Canada Inc.
329 March Road, Suite 232, Box 11
Kanata, Ontario K2K 2E1   Tel.: (613) 599-0878

Arbitration and Mediation Institute of Ontario Inc.
234 Eglinton Avenue East, Suite 303
Toronto, Ontario M4P 1K5   Tel.: (416) 487-4447

Society for Professionals in Dispute Resolution
National Office
1730 Rhode Island Avenue N.W., Suite 909
Washington, D.C. 20036, U.S.A.   Tel.: (202) 833-2188

Preparing for ADR

2

Key Concepts

Preparation for ADR includes:

*   understanding all the relevant aspects of one's case
*   setting goals and objectives for each ADR process contemplated
*   planning a strategy and back-up plan to achieve those goals
*   clarifying the roles of counsel and client
*   understanding the process that will be utilized
*   anticipating tactics and techniques
*   analyzing the strengths and weaknesses of one's case
*   understanding the opposing counsel and client's case and preferred style
*   putting together a brief summary of the relevant issues and documents

1. COMPREHENSIVE FILE REVIEW

In preparing for any form of ADR, a full review of the case file is required. This comprehensive review can be categorized under three areas: information, strategy and constraints.

Information: To prepare for any form of ADR, counsel must understand all the events leading up to the dispute and the chronological legal steps such as claims by the parties, counterclaims, motions, relief requested and the status of the lawsuit. Relevant documents need to be gathered. These may include physician's notes, hospital records, photographs, discovery transcripts, contracts, leases, policies, verification of lost wages and surveillance evidence. Counsel

31

needs to consider which information should be disclosed to the other side and which needs to be maintained as confidential. The strategic ADR advocate reviews all important documents including correspondence, history of demands and offers to settle. A review of the relevant case law may affect the strategic choice of ADR options and should, for that reason, also be considered.

Strategy: Part of strategizing appropriately for ADR is setting goals and objectives, considering the format of the ADR process including whether a pre-ADR meeting is required, and considering the status of negotiations to date and the preferred negotiation style and tactics of the other counsel. Setting ADR goals and objectives is very similar to the process of setting evidentiary goals in the litigation process. Typical ADR goals may include:

- pursuing constructive settlement discussions;
- gathering information about the file, including information about the other party, supporting documents and additional facts about the file;
- opportunity to persuasively set out one's case analysis directly to the other client without the filter of counsel;
- opportunity for clients to meet face to face in a safe, neutral setting;
- compliance with mandated process requirements in programs such as the specialized tribunals and court-connected ADR programs; and
- opportunity to allow experts to meet and discuss, informally and without prejudice, the merits of the case.

It is very important to consider why a client is being taken to ADR and/or why counsel is being encouraged to pursue it so that relevant information can be gathered and an appropriate strategy formulated to maximize the utility of the process.

In determining a strategy to maximize the ADR process, it is important to consider the formats available. Formats can include pre-ADR meetings, telephone conferences, joint meetings and separate meetings with the selected third party intervenor. For example, in the insurance context, a pre-ADR meeting between joint defendants or between counsel to set out the parameters for negotiation, mediation or arbitration serves a number of strategic purposes. It provides an opportunity to gather facts and documents, determine allocation of liability and consider a unified approach in dealing with the plaintiff. This can be done cost-effectively by telephone conference call and may dramatically reduce the time needed at the actual ADR session. The stage of litigation and the status of negotiations to date will inform advocates as to the utility of a pre-ADR meeting.

Strategic consideration of who will participate in the ADR session and the nature of their roles can be a defining factor in the success of achieving ADR goals. The format of the mediation session may include considerations of the sequence in which documentation will be presented, whether documents may be initially withheld or not, the need for separate meeting rooms, and adequate telephone access. ADR advocates are increasingly using visual aids such as Power

Point presentations and videotapes, so equipment should be available for this purpose.

Constraints: The two main constraints in doing a comprehensive file review are limitations on authority to settle, and time limits. Some ADR advocates confirm the limits of settlement authority with the client in writing. If there are multiple clients, meeting with them to determine the limits verbally and confirming later in writing may also be of use. Considerations with regard to authority to settle are pivotal to determining ADR goals and strategies. There may be personal or organizational deadlines to be considered. These may apply to the ADR advocates themselves, to their clients, or to the representatives or clients on the other side. Critical dates include discovery dates, case management dates and trial dates. The strategic advocate may consider creating or imposing time constraints in order to move the parties more quickly to settlement discussions or to elicit necessary documents. The effective ADR advocate also gives consideration to hidden agendas or underlying interests which may motivate the parties. A comprehensive discussion of interests in the context of negotiation is included at pp. 45-7.

2. CLARIFYING THE ROLES OF COUNSEL AND CLIENT

Part of the strategic preparation for ADR is deciding who should attend the mediation session. Ideally, in a mediation, counsel and a client with sufficient information to fully participate in the settlement discussions and the authority to settle should be present. Occasionally, ADR advocates may require witnesses to attend the session and may use experts. Experts would include corporate in-house professionals or structured settlement experts. The use of experts in mediation is discussed at p. 90.

3. ADVISING THE CLIENT

The client needs to be aware of the nature of the ADR process, including whether the ADR is voluntary or mandated by a court or tribunal. Clients need to understand the stages of the negotiation, mediation or arbitration process and the roles of all the different participants. Pre-ADR preparation of the client includes a discussion of individual meetings, the confidentiality and without prejudice nature of some forms of ADR, and the different roles of the participants in mediation and arbitration. Clients need to understand that they may voluntarily terminate the mediation at any time. It is useful to canvass the mediation agreement's content with the client so that he or she understands the nature of confidentiality, the fact that mediators are not compellable as witnesses regarding disclosure made in ADR proceedings, the neutral's fees, and arrangements for payment for ADR services.

In the case of mediation, clients need to understand the different formats that mediation may take and the fact that mediations may be less formal than adjudicative processes such as arbitration. Advocates should inform their clients that these formats may include parties and counsel speaking directly with each other, with or without the mediator present, and that there is a possibility of counsel meeting with each other without their clients. The role of the mediator may be very familiar to institutional clients such as insurers. However, this may be a very new process for the plaintiff client. ADR advocates should describe the mediator's background, experience and qualifications, as well as the fact that mediators have a duty to be neutral and impartial with respect to the parties and the subject-matter of the dispute. The parties need to understand that the mediator does not provide legal advice and does not make a determination of right or wrong. The role of the mediator is to facilitate communication among the parties, identify the issues in dispute, share information among the parties, and explore options for settlement. The mediator may also focus the discussion and control any emotional outbursts from the parties. The mediator, as process manager, chairs the discussions and clarifies communication, and he or she may make suggestions for settlement and coach the parties in negotiating a settlement. Clients should be aware that mediators are ethically bound not to disclose any information received in confidence during the mediation. They need to understand that there may be waiting periods while the mediator meets with the other side. Rather than this being a source of frustration, if the separate meetings are discussed in advance, clients will understand that this is not an indication of mediator bias.

Role of the ADR advocate: While many clients will be very familiar with the ADR process, some participants will have a pre-determined view of the advocate's role. It is imperative that the client understand that the advocate's role might differ, depending on the particular model of mediation adopted. For example, in facilitative mediations, the role of the advocate may be to obtain the best possible resolution for the client by participating in respectful conversation. This role may necessitate more of a problem-solving format where strengths and weaknesses of the case are discussed. The expression of empathy towards the opposing party or counsel will be common, and discussion of case law may or may not occur. In an evaluative mediation format, while the goal may still be to obtain the best possible resolution for the client, the relative strengths and weaknesses of the parties' cases will be the focus of discussion. Relevant case law will be discussed, and the approach to the problem may be legalistic and rights-based. In a session such as this, more traditional courtroom skills are utilized. Clients should know that they have the option of speaking to their representatives at any time during the mediation process, regardless of what process is adopted. They also need to understand that they will bear the ultimate decision-making authority regarding whether to accept a set of options or a settlement proposal. If settlement is reached, the ADR advocate will likely work with opposing counsel to draft an agreement or minutes of settlement.

Client's role: In many forms of ADR such as direct negotiation and mediation, the client will play a direct role in the session. The client needs to be advised of this expectation in advance. Close attention should be paid to discussing the client's expected level of participation. During mediation, questions or comments are often directed to the client. The client should understand that he or she does not need to verbally respond. Strategically, clients should appear interested throughout the session even if they remain silent.

If the ADR advocate wishes to have the client participate orally in the presentation of the case, the division of responsibility between the lawyer and the client should be arranged in advance. There should be a discussion as to what aspects of the case the client will share and whether the client will be commenting on documents. Many ADR advocates reassure their clients that they need not respond to any questions they do not feel comfortable addressing. The client needs to understand typical mediation ground rules and should be rehearsed in speaking directly to the mediator and the other parties and in making an effort to appear forthright and credible. It is important to advise the client not to be argumentative and to avoid hostility to the extent possible. The author notes that many ADR advocates in the insurance context prepare their clients to behave as if before a jury, and to tell their story sincerely and in a straightforward manner.

The ADR advocate will also review with the client the location of the mediation or arbitration, and where the client should meet his or her representatives prior to the session commencing. Clients further need to know the appropriate attire for a mediation or arbitration and the estimated length of the session. Lastly, as previously mentioned, any limits pertaining to settlement authority are ideally provided in writing prior to the ADR session.

4. PREPARING TO BE AN EFFECTIVE ADVOCATE IN NEGOTIATION AND MEDIATION

Experienced advocates strategically plan each negotiation and mediation. The following is a list of questions to be considered in preparing to participate effectively in a direct negotiation or mediated settlement discussion. These questions are also included in a checklist in Appendix 2.2 at the end of this chapter.

What are the issues in dispute? Advocates should define the dispute in clear, concise and straightforward language. Any settlement implementation problems should be considered during the preparatory stage. Likewise, any issues in dispute which require further information should be noted. Issues may be organized as procedural, psychological or substantive in nature.

Who are the parties? When considering the appropriate parties in the ADR session, consider the client's spouse, children, and any trusted friends or financial advisors. These individuals may be influential in terms of reaching and/or reviewing any settlement. The representatives themselves may have senior partners or work within teams which will influence strategy, approach and reaching an agreement. Bear in mind that an individual absent from the ADR session can still be influencing the parties at the table. Therefore, ensure that all appropriate parties are present or accessible.

What are the facts relevant to resolving the problem? Advocates should possess a thorough, working knowledge of the chronology of the dispute and the salient facts relevant to settlement discussions. The areas of discussion in a negotiation or mediation are not limited to the jurisdiction of a court, so advocates need to consider any facts which may persuade the other side to sympathize with their client's viewpoint.

Is there any additional information or documentation which the other side does not have which could be shared with the other parties and/or the mediator? Disputes are dynamic, and circumstances continue to change. The sharing of information can have a persuasive effect on the views of the other side and can provide the impetus to consider different settlement options. In considering the evidence to be submitted during the session, think about whether there is any other information (*e.g.*, costings, changes in circumstances, etc.) which will influence the other party's decision to reach an agreement. Sharing information is also a way of expressing commitment to participate in the process in good faith and to resolve the problem. Ask whether data is available concerning the client's out-of-pocket expenses and whether there is documentation to substantiate any damages at this point in time.

What are the positions of the various parties? While interest-based negotiation will ideally maximize results, it is always prudent to consider the positions, rights and entitlements of all the parties.

What are the interests/needs/concerns of all the parties? Interests are the basis for any individual action. Interests may include personal, professional, economic, psychological and business considerations: see pp. 46-7. Principled negotiation is premised on considering the underlying motivations, concerns and needs of all the parties in order to form a foundation for a mutually acceptable solution. Remember that representatives and advocates may also have interests or hidden agendas which propel the dispute. Further, consider the interests of those parties who are not at the table but may influence any terms of settlement.

What are the alternatives to a negotiated/mediated settlement? Part of any strategic negotiation analysis is a consideration of the alternatives. This reality check should be canvassed with the client in advance so that the parties are clear as to what possible results or process steps are available should the negotiations flounder.

What options are available to resolve the situation? Prior to any negotiation or mediation, possible options for resolution should be canvassed with the client. This investigation prepares the parties for settlement and allows creative brainstorming to take place in advance of the meeting. Ask the client to be innovative and to reverse his or her assumptions and roles. In a negotiated or mediated settlement, many ideas can be transformed into settlement options which would be outside the jurisdiction of a trier of fact.

Is there anything which should be considered in finalizing an agreement? The parties may, at times, require outside authorization in respect of a proposed resolution. For example, an insurance company may require a second signature or authorization from a higher level in some situations. A non-profit board may require the ratification of its members. Time constraints and the impact of governing legislation can also be considerations in finalizing an agreement.

5. PREPARATION OF ADR BRIEF

The use of mediation and arbitration briefs will be discussed in Chapters 4 and 5 respectively. Mediation briefs have been referred to as mediation memoranda or synopses of loss. Effective advocates exercise judgment as to what is required in each indvidual case. Due consideration should be paid to the amount of time the advocate wishes to spend preparing the brief and the amount of information he or she wishes to disclose.

Following are the components of a mediation brief. A checklist of them is to be found in Appendix 2.3.

Identify the parties and their representatives: It is very important to identify the parties and the legal counsel for the plaintiff and the defendant. Very often, a short style of cause is used on the title page or at the beginning of the brief. Some mediation briefs identify the names of counsel both for the mediation session and the trial. This may be useful information if those names are different. Addresses, phone numbers and facsimile numbers for the representatives should also be included.

Court file number: In the case of mandated mediation in a court or tribunal, or a private mediation where the case has been filed in court, the court file number is a useful, unique, identifying number. Many ADR practitioners have multiple files, and use of the court file number is just a further way of identifying the brief and reducing confusion.

Statement of issues: The statement of issues is an indication both to the mediator and to the other parties of what will be important to the submitting party at the mediation session. This statement should be brief. It should also be kept in mind that the plaintiff and the defendant will possibly submit different statements of the issues. In the practice of mediation, this is not an unusual scenario and very often is an indication of the reasons for convening the mediation in the first instance.

Factual and legal issues in dispute: Some counsel have used the title "Factual and Legal Issues in Dispute" to further delineate the nature of the issues and to present them in an organized fashion. This is just a helpful way to make the brief easy and quick to read and understand.

Parties' positions and interests: Given that mediation is described as an interest-based process, many counsel include the party's legal position as well as a brief description of their client's needs and concerns which they would like to see addressed at the mediation. As will be discussed more completely in Chapters 3 and 4, client interests include business, professional, personal and economic concerns as well as legal considerations.

Attached documents: In this section of the brief, the parties generally include relevant documents. The general guideline here is: What documents do the other parties and the ADR intervenor need in order to understand the case, and what documents would assist in moving the parties forward in their settlement discussions? In the case of insurance files, typical documents would include a copy of the statement of claim if any, a copy of the statement of defence if any, a copy of the policy in question, medical reports and records, correspondence, costings or basis for specific damages, and documentation verifying out-of-pocket losses.

Date, time and location of the mediation: A brief should include the name of the mediator and the time, date and location of the mediation as a further way of identifying the brief.

When producing a mediation brief, advocates should consider the cost of putting together a complex brief in conjunction with the value of the file and the economic circumstances of the client. The amount of information and the number of documents provided will have a direct impact on how successful the mediation is. Those preparing mediation briefs should consider what the other parties and the mediator need to know in order to have a full and constructive discussion at the mediation session.

Summary

A pre-ADR review includes an analysis of all the facts and issues relevant to the dispute as well as consideration of strategy and of any constraints on the conduct of the session. ADR advocates should consider rehearsing with the client if the client is to participate in the mediation. At the very least, the advocate should ensure that the client fully understands the roles of all the participants at the ADR session. Preparing a pre-ADR brief such as a mediation memorandum may be helpful to outline the circumstances and history of the dispute with the mediator and the other side. This pre-ADR exchange of relevant information and documentation will expedite the conduct of the session. Setting ADR goals and objectives will inform the advocate as to how best to utilize the ADR process and work with the intervenor in order to achieve the goals of the client.

APPENDIX 2.1
COUNSEL AND CLIENT MEDIATION PREPARATION CHECKLIST[1]

COUNSEL

☐ Conduct a comprehensive file review:

    ☐ Gather all information and documents;

    ☐ Consider strategic choices and set mediation goals;

---

[1] For a discussion of these points, see pp. 31-5.

    ☐   Consider what constraints there may be on pursuing settlement or resolution.

☐ Determine who will attend the mediation and whether experts will need to be involved.

☐ Prepare the client.

☐ Prepare an opening statement.

CLIENT

☐ Ensure that the client understands the nature and the process of mediation.

☐ Ensure that the client understands the role of the mediator.

☐ Prepare the client as to his or her role in presenting the case and participating in the mediation.

☐ Ensure that the client understands that he or she needs to present as credible and sincere.

☐ Ensure that the client is prepared to hear the presentation by the other party.

☐ Ensure that the client is aware of the date, time and location of the mediation as well as any contingency plan in case of problems.

APPENDIX 2.2
EFFECTIVE NEGOTIATION AND MEDIATION CHECKLIST[2]

☐ What are the issues in dispute?

☐ Who are the parties?

☐ What are the facts relevant to resolving the problem?

☐ Is there any additional information or documentation which the other side does not have which could be shared with the other parties and/or the mediator?

☐ What are the positions of the various parties?

☐ What are the interests/needs/concerns of all the parties?

☐ What are the alternatives to a negotiated/mediated settlement?

☐ What options are available to resolve the situation?

☐ Is there anything that should be considered in finalizing an agreement, *e.g.*, authorization, input from experts such as accountants, personal advisors, legal advisors, etc.?

---

[2] For a discussion of these points, see pp. 35-7.

APPENDIX 2.3
CHECKLIST OF COMPONENTS OF A MEDIATION BRIEF[3]

☐　names of the parties and their representatives

☐　court file number (if applicable)

☐　statement of issues

☐　factual and legal issues in dispute

☐　parties' positions and interests

☐　list of documents

☐　date, time and location of the mediation

APPENDIX 2.4
SUGGESTIONS FOR DRAFTING SETTLEMENT DOCUMENTS

☐　Use plain English.

☐　Identify people by their full names.

☐　Specify dates.

☐　Answer who, what, where, when and how.

☐　Document any agreement in principle.

☐　List each key provision separately.

☐　Specify the method and details of any payment.

☐　Omit any mention of blame, fault or guilt.

☐　Consider the need for confidentiality.

☐　Expressly set out expectations and obligations, especially in the case of conditional or interim agreements.

☐　Consider what will happen if the agreement is not fulfilled.

☐　Bring sample clauses with you to the ADR for on-the-spot drafting.

---

[3]　For a discussion of these points, see pp. 37-8.

Part B

ADR Core Concepts
and Skills

Negotiation

> ## Key Concepts

- Negotiation is the most commonly used form of dispute resolution in the insurance industry.

- Understanding negotiation theory and concepts is fundamental to strategic planning and advocacy preparation.

- The two primary negotiation models used in the insurance industry are the competitive/positional model and the problem-solving/co-operative/interest-based/principled model.

- "Positions" are rigid stances based on the parties' assessment of their rights.

- "Interests" include the underlying wants, needs, desires and concerns which motivate the parties' positions.

- Positional bargaining is characterized by an emphasis on rights and a pro-posal/counter-proposal approach to exchanging offers.

- Interest-based negotiation focuses on mutual gain and consideration of the parties' underlying needs and concerns.

- Effective negotiators may be aggressive or co-operative in their approach.

- Effective advocates recognize both their own personal negotiation style and the negotiating behaviours of the other parties.

- Negotiation tactics, techniques and models can be adapted to personal advo-cacy preferences.

1. NEGOTIATION PRIMER

Negotiation has been characterized as the "pre-eminent form of dispute resolution".[1] This characterization is certainly true in the insurance context. Given the nature of insurance disputes, which typically involve an individual plaintiff and an institutional defendant, the parties are often motivated to seek resolution directly with each other.

Negotiation has been defined as any form of direct or indirect communication whereby parties who have opposing interests discuss the form of any joint action which they might take to manage and ultimately resolve the dispute between them.[2] In a negotiation, there is significant opportunity for flexibility since the actual terms of the agreement are concluded by the parties themselves and can be as broad or as specific as the parties desire.

Another definition of negotiation is the "art and science of persuasion".[3] This characterization applies to situations in which two or more parties recognize that differences of interest and values exist among them and that compromise agreement should ideally be sought through negotiation. This particular definition recognizes the personal style or art of the negotiator as well as the science, models or techniques which a negotiator uses to pursue his or her objectives. This chapter enlarges upon these two concepts as they apply to negotiation in the insurance industry.

Effective negotiation allows the parties to agree to an outcome which is mutually satisfactory. Often a negotiated settlement is recorded in the form of an agreement which, once signed, has the force of a contract between the parties. If the settlement is negotiated in the context of a litigious dispute, then the parties may wish to register the settlement with a court in conformity with the applicable court's rules of practice.

2. NEGOTIATION MODELS

Two primary negotiation models used in the insurance industry are:

(1) competitive/positional; and
(2) problem-solving/co-operative/interest-based/principled.

It should be noted that effective negotiators are able to move easily between the models, resulting in a hybrid of the two.

---

[1] S.G. Goldberg, E.A. Frank and N.H. Rogers, *Dispute Resolution: Negotiation, Mediation and Other Processes*, 2nd ed. (Boston: Little, Brown and Company, 1992).
[2] The Law Society of Upper Canada, *Short Glossary of Dispute Resolution Terms* (Toronto: Law Society of Upper Canada, 1992).
[3] Howard Raissa, *The Art and Science of Negotiation – How to Resolve Conflict and Get the Best Out of Bargaining* (Boston, Mass.: Harvard University Press, 1982).

(a) Competitive/Positional Negotiation

In the competitive model of negotiation, the parties attempt to maximize their returns at the expense of one another. They assume adversarial stances or positions and only consider themselves successful if the other parties "lose". Other terms used to describe competitive/positional negotiation are "win-lose" and "zero sum" negotiations. This model is often used in distributive problems where a finite resource is distributed among the parties, resulting in one party "winning" everything and the other party "losing" all of the stakes. The goal is to win or recover most of the fixed amount of assets or resources.

Competitive bargaining has been criticized because it focuses on specific positions rather than attempting to discern the true interests of the parties. This can promote brinkmanship, and it can discourage mutual trust which is necessary for joint gain. At any point during positional negotiations, one party may decide to use a variety of tactics in order to obtain an advantage over another. This behaviour can include pressure tactics (attempting to force the other party to accept specific terms), intimidation (implicit or explicit), deliberate ambiguity regarding the scope of the negotiating mandate, and blatantly unethical behaviour such as providing misleading or false information.[4]

Another notable characteristic of the competitive/positional model is the use of evaluative statements during negotiation discussions. This model is premised on the strengths or weaknesses of a particular position. As a result, the negotiators must persuade the others that their position is more "correct". This persuasion can be accomplished through evaluations made by the negotiators concerning the merits of their own case and/or the strengths and weaknesses of the other side's position. Commonly, insurance disputes arise because a claim has been denied, there has been an allegation of professional misconduct, or there is a dispute about the application of the wording of the policy. All these types of substantive disputes can lend themselves to an evaluative framework where the nature of the dispute can be assessed in light of the applicable legislation, policies, precedents, and other rights-based information.

(b) Problem-Solving/Co-operative/Interest-Based/Principled Model

Co-operative or problem-solving negotiation starts from the premise that the gains of one party need not be at the expense of the other party. In the co-operative/interest-based negotiation model, common and individual interests and values are explored and stressed. The use of objective standards such as time frames, expert analysis or legal precedent are used to benchmark the progress of the negotiation and to assist in narrowing the options. The goal of the negotiation is to find a solution which is fair and mutually agreeable to the parties.

---

[4] Uri and Patton Fisher, *Getting to Yes* (Boston: Houghton Mifflin, 1981). See also Thomas R. Colosi, *On and Off the Record: Colosi on Negotiation* (Dubuque, Iowa: Kendall/Hunt Publishing Company, 1993).

Over the past two decades, a form of co-operative negotiation known as principled negotiation[5] has gained widespread acceptance. Principled negotiation encompasses four basic points:

(1) people;
(2) interests;
(3) options; and
(4) objective criteria.

Principled negotiation encourages the negotiators to "separate the people from the problem".[6] While the people are sometimes the problem, this model espouses concentrating on the dispute at hand rather than succumbing to intimidation or personal attacks.

A hallmark of the principled negotiation method is the exploration and consideration of interests. As previously noted, interests refer to the underlying needs and concerns of the parties. In many disputes, including insurance negotiation, those interests include the interests of the clients and those of their representatives. Interests may be procedural, psychological or substantive. For example, an institutional client may have a procedural interest in completing the negotiation and closing the file before year-end. One of the negotiators may have a psychological interest in demonstrating to the client his or her prowess or value as a professional negotiator. An insurance company may have a substantive interest in ensuring settlement within the reserves allocated for the file. Another kind of substantive interest might be the need of the plaintiff to be reimbursed for out-of-pocket expenses incurred after being injured in an accident.

Interests can be classified in the following categories:

(a) personal;
(b) professional;
(c) organizational;
(d) economic; and
(e) legal.

A personal interest, particularly in the insurance context, may include the need of a claims adjuster to demonstrate fairness and reasonableness in the management of corporate assets. A plaintiff in a slip and fall case may have a personal interest in ensuring that this kind of accident does not recur. A useful illustration of a professional interest is the situation where legal counsel has a need to show opposing counsel that he or she is a sophisticated, competent and credible advocate. An organizational need may be ensuring that benefits paid out in a particular set of circumstances are consistent with past and future payouts. Economic interests are widely applicable and can include the cost of legal representation, the cost of time spent pursuing the dispute, loss of income for the

---

[5] Uri and Patton Fisher, *op. cit.*, p. 11.
[6] *Ibid.*

plaintiff, loss of productive work time for the institutional client, and the unpredictability of any economic damage award at trial. With regard to legalities, in an interest-based insurance negotiation, legal precedents or risk analysis of one's case may be factors in motivating ultimate settlement discussions.

The principled negotiation approach, also referred to as the "getting to yes" model, focuses on generating multiple and creative options for resolving the situation. The goal is to generate a variety of settlement possibilities or solutions prior to the parties committing to a given solution or combination of options. This approach encourages the parties to brainstorm for many options for resolution, be they reasonable or unreasonable. The possibilities are subsequently evaluated. In this way, with a greater number of settlement options, the parties may be more likely to arrive at a final set of settlement outcomes.

The use of objective criteria should be a yardstick for measuring which options may be acceptable to one or more of the parties. According to the proponents of principled negotiation, an objective standard is often considered as the "hard" aspect of an otherwise "soft" process. Objective standards, in the context of insurance disputes, can include the applicable insurance legislation, insurance case law, policies, specific economic loss/risk assessments, etc.

Proponents of principled bargaining believe that bargaining over fixed positions can lead to situations where the parties will either be inflexible (hard bargaining) or accept unilateral losses (soft bargaining) in order to reach an agreement. In contrast, use of co-operative or principled bargaining, which attempts to reconcile the underlying needs and concerns of all the parties, gives the negotiators a framework within which to reach agreement and to circumvent the potential problems associated with hard and soft bargaining.

3. NEGOTIATION PROCESS

Each negotiation has its own unique characteristics. There is no uniform or exclusive manner of conducting a bargaining session. For example, the timing of an offer and the question of which party should make the first offer are within the negotiator's discretion and are determined by the overall dynamics of the particular negotiation.

There are five generic stages in any given negotiation, whether positional or interest-based:

(1) invitation to negotiate and building rapport;
(2) clarification of the issues and setting a mutual agenda;
(3) exchange of information and consideration of underlying interests;
(4) generation of options; and
(5) coming to an agreement.

Invitation to negotiate and building rapport: This step is often neglected or overlooked even though dialogue to persuade another party to consider resolution must always be initiated by someone. To have a satisfying and effective negotiation, it is imperative that the negotiators speak to one another and build rapport in advance of the formal session. The author has observed that negotiation discussions are more likely to be amicable and productive where the parties have:

- spoken to each other before the negotiation either by telephone or in a face-to-face meeting;
- established a prior professional relationship, often from work conducted on a previous file;
- drafted correspondence to the other prior to the negotiations; or
- exchanged a few words at the beginning of the face-to-face meeting.

Very often, erroneous assumptions have been made about the opposing party. These can be readily corrected during this introductory stage. This stage also provides an important opportunity to assess the negotiating style of the opposing party with a view to informing one's own persuasive strategy. Negotiation style will be discussed later in this chapter.

Clarification of the issues and setting a mutual agenda: Very often in negotiations the parties possess radically different views of the issues in dispute. The first step in the negotiation process is to clarify the substantive issues. It is not uncommon for one party to have identified two issues, whereas the other identifies seven. Negotiators need to ensure that their counterpart has a comprehensive understanding of what the issues are. The negotiators need to work together to set an agenda in order to ensure that the issues of all the parties are fully canvassed.

Exchange of information and consideration of underlying interests: This stage is fundamental to any successful negotiation. Most of the time, the parties do not have a mutual understanding of the facts surrounding the dispute. Time must be spent ensuring that all the parties have a mutual understanding of the material facts. Work during this stage involves presenting one's own information and listening to that offered by the other side. Many negotiations fail to settle because there is either a lack of information for making an informed agreement or there is a perception that important information has been withheld or is otherwise lacking. There is an abundance of information which can be strategically shared at this stage and will assist the other side in making a decision about pursuing negotiation discussions and/or committing to a resolution.

In competitive/positional bargaining, this stage may not include direct discussion or reference to the underlying needs and concerns of the parties. In a competitive/positional model, the parties present their positions to each other, with supporting rationale, in the hope of persuading the other side to adopt their point of view. In the co-operative/interest-based model, the parties may ask open-ended questions about the other party's motivations and offer information about the needs and concerns of their own side. In the insurance context, the exploration of interests can be done concurrently with the parties asking questions of each other about the case. At this stage, relevant documents may also be exchanged to further elucidate or clarify each party's view of the situation.

Generation of options: In either negotiation model, the parties need to discuss possible ways to reach resolution. This discussion may include generating ideas, solutions, options or further procedural steps. Compare the potential options generated in a long-term disability file with those identified in a municipal slip and fall case:

Options – Long-Term Disability

- continuation of the disability benefits;
- provision of updated medical information;
- evaluation of the complainant by an independent medical examiner;
- provision of receipts or documentation validating out-of-pocket costs;
- payment by the insurance company of rehabilitation or other adjunct health services;
- payment of a lump sum to close the file and discontinue benefits in the future;
- discontinuation of the lawsuit on consent;
- other economic compensation such as lawyers' fees, prejudgment interest and disbursements; and/or
- discontinuation of settlement discussions and pursuit of legal proceedings.

Options – Occupier's Liability

- compensation for damages;
- provision of updated medical information;
- evaluation of the complainant by an independent medical examiner;
- provision of receipts or documentation validating out-of-pocket costs;
- payment by the insurance company of rehabilitation or other adjunct health services;
- payment of a lump sum to close the file;
- discontinuation of the lawsuit on consent;
- other economic compensation such as lawyers' fees, prejudgment interest and disbursements;
- discontinuation of settlement discussions and pursuit of legal proceedings;
- review of the municipality's policy for sanding and clearing the streets in a Canadian winter;
- arranging to speak to a municipal public joint citizen's liaison group about recommendations for assisting the elderly in the winter; and/or
- compensation for the plaintiff's loss of opportunity to take a trip to Florida as a direct result of the slip and fall.

While these lists are not exhaustive, they do exemplify the range and types of options which might be considered by the negotiating parties alone or together.

The examples also demonstrate the potential differences between positional and interest-based negotiations. The options for resolving a long-term disability claim, set out in the first column, exemplify the types of options which would be generated in a positional/competitive type of bargaining session. The options for the slip and fall, outlined in the second column, identify virtually the same options as in the long-term disability case, along with additional options addressing the plaintiff's specific needs and some of the needs of the municipality. In either model, various options must be considered for use in ultimately customizing a proposal or offer by either party.

Coming to an agreement: Even where there is tremendous rapport between the negotiators, a clear exchange of ideas with which both parties are in agreement, and a brilliant list of settlement options, the negotiation will not be successful unless the parties are able to reach an agreement. Reaching agreement can occur in a number of ways. In the typical positional/competitive model, the parties will often use a proposal/counter-proposal type of bargaining. In this model, one party develops a proposal and presents it to the other side. The other side responds by way of a counter-proposal. In this way, both parties put a without prejudice commitment on the table as to what they will settle for at this point in time. Very often, these two positions are quite far apart. This can negatively affect the negotiators' trust in each other's motives and can detract from their commitment to continue to discuss the issues in good faith. In the author's experience, it takes a minimum of four offers to settle an insurance file. This includes a proposal by one party, a counter-proposal by the other, and then several modified proposals before mutual acceptance is achieved. Often the parties need more information, or they need to be able to assess the options generated against some kind of objective standard, before finalizing an offer. As previously mentioned, in the insurance context the objective standards commonly used include reports or opinions by experts, legal precedents, industry practice and/or verification of specific economic loss.

In both the interest-based/co-operative and the positional/competitive models, the parties must assess their ability to accept any given option. The parties may evaluate their proposals and the progress of the negotiation in light of their B.A.T.N.A. (best alternative to a negotiated agreement).[7] The B.A.T.N.A. is "the standard against which any proposed agreement should be measured". It is, in essence, the best of all the possible alternatives to negotiation should the latter fail. In an interest-based or principled negotiation, the parties actively consider the alternatives in evaluating their ability to accept an agreement.

A further factor which should be considered in coming to an agreement is the mandate or authority of the negotiators to settle. Clarifying the authority to come to a commitment is extremely important when acting on a client's behalf. All issues pertaining to settlement authority should be reviewed and accepted prior

---

[7] *Ibid.*, p. 100.

to the negotiation. This practice avoids the situation where settlement authority is a bar to reaching an agreement at the final stage of the negotiation.

While the conceptual negotiation framework may include the steps just outlined, a negotiation in its simplest form is a conversation between two individuals. This conversation may take place over the phone or in a face-to-face meeting. In the case of insurance files, the conversation may also include clients and/or lawyers. It should be considered that these negotiations are ongoing and may be interrupted from time to time. For example, one party may send a letter with a proposal. The other party might respond by telephone or by letter. The parties could get together and discuss the issues and exchange some documents. At a later date, they might pick up the phone again and make another proposal. Negotiation is very unstructured and flexible, and the process is entirely within the mutual control of the parties.

4. NEGOTIATION STYLE

Advocates should consider their own negotiation style as well as the approaches adopted by their negotiation counterpart. The negotiation literature speaks to five styles of conflict resolution:[8]

(1) withdrawal/avoidance;
(2) smoothing/accommodation;
(3) compromise;
(4) forcing/competition; and
(5) problem-solving or collaboration.

Withdrawal/avoidance: This conflict resolution style is self-descriptive. It refers to those individuals who maintain neutrality at all costs and ignore conflict in the hope that it will go away. These "conflict avoiders" remove themselves physically or mentally from the situation and feel little concern for accomplishing a resolution. They usually have a great desire not to be involved. This conflict strategy can be effective in insurance cases where the issues are trivial, the cost/benefit analysis indicates that the potential losses outweigh the potential gains, and there is not enough time to properly work through the issues involved. One drawback to using a withdrawal or avoidance approach is that it may only delay an inevitable confrontation.

Smoothing/accommodation: Accommodators feel a greater concern for the relationship with the parties in the dispute than for resolution of the issues. Sometimes accommodators will smooth over or ignore the conflict in order to keep everyone happy. They see open conflict as destructive and would rather give in to the will of the others than disrupt the peace. A smoothing or accommodating strategy might be used in the insurance context when the issues are relatively

---

[8] James G. Patterson, *How to Become a Better Negotiator* (Toronto, Ont.: Amacom, American Management Association, 1996), p. 25.

minor, damage to the relationship will hurt all the parties involved, there is a need to temporarily reduce the level of conflict in order to get more information, and emotions are running too high to effectively progress. In the long term, a completely smoothing or accommodating style may offer only a temporary solution and not deal with the real issues. Also, the concerns of the accommodating party are often not satisfied.

Compromise: A basic characteristic of the compromising style is the assumption that everyone has a full right to express opinions. The compromiser's style is to look for solutions that everyone can live with, possibly using a democratic method such as voting as a way of avoiding direct conflict. Compromisers believe that a high-quality solution optimal to one party is not as important as a solution which all the parties can accept. A compromising strategy is useful when both parties will gain something in a compromise, a temporary solution is required for a complex problem, and both parties have relatively equal bargaining power. Compromise may not be the preferred method where the parties wish to move beyond a "zero sum" or "win-lose" characterization of the case. Compromise perpetuates positional-type bargaining and may not leave opportunity to "expand the pie" and look for broader solutions. There is a view in the dispute resolution literature that compromise does not necessarily produce the best or optimal solution for all the parties.

Forcing/competition: Adopting a competitive style may involve the view that reaching one's own goals is more important than meeting the objectives of all the participants. Competitors may also employ power tactics to obtain their demands. This type of negotiator perpetuates the win-lose characterization of the conflict, one in which someone must lose and someone must win. Those who use the forcing/competitive style have great respect for their own personal and professional power, and they may be inclined to submit to a power-based process such as arbitration. Forcing or competition can be effective when the parties require an immediate decision, all the parties appreciate the use of power and force, and the disputants understand and accept the power relationship and dynamics between them. In negative terms, a competitive or forcing style may result in the true cause of the conflict remaining unexplored and unresolved. This reality can adversely impact the longevity of any agreement reached.

Problem-solving or collaboration: The problem-solving or collaborative strategist considers the individuals involved in the negotiation and the desired results. Conflict is viewed as optimally handled through open and honest communication. This negotiator attempts to achieve group consensus and is willing to spend time in order to achieve agreement. The problem-solving or collaborative approach is effective when everyone in the conflict is familiar with the message, the parties have common goals or mutual ground they can rely upon, and the conflict results from a lack of information or communication between the parties. The difficulty with the problem-solving or collaborative approach is that it does not work with people who have different goals or values. If the opposing negotiator is determined to use power, problem-solving may not be effective. Likewise, the problem-solving approach is time-consuming and, when a group or a situation requires a fast decision, a forcing style may be preferred.

Effective negotiators analyze their particular preference for dealing with conflict and recognize that they make different choices in different contexts. Negotiators who represent others, *e.g.*, advocates for lawsuit claimants or insurance companies, need to also consider the style preferred by their client. This is particularly important if the client is to be involved in the negotiation process. Likewise, negotiators should consider the style preference of their opposing negotiator. Just as the problem-solving approach may not be effective with a forcing/competitive negotiator, a forcing/competitive negotiator may have tremendous difficulty with an avoider. The moral of the story is that negotiators need to consider all aspects of their own and their counterpart's style and be prepared to modify their preferred style in order to achieve an optimal result.

5. BEYOND BASICS

(a) Characteristics of Effective Negotiators

Studies have shown that distinct approaches to negotiation exist, each with a different set of negotiation characteristics.[9] Two of the patterns of negotiation which have been identified in the literature are directly applicable in the insurance industry. These are the co-operative approach and the aggressive approach. No one pattern is effective in all situations, so the effective advocate should understand the traits exhibited by both the co-operative and the aggressive negotiator.

Traits of the co-operative negotiator: The co-operative negotiator is seen as trustworthy, ethical, courteous and sincere. The effective co-operative negotiator relies on reasonable opening positions, evaluates the case in a realistic manner, and does not use threats, coercion or other tactics. There is a willingness to share information and to use excellent communication skills in order to explore the opponent's position and interests.

The ineffective co-operative negotiator shares the traits of honesty, trustworthiness and courteousness, but may be excessively obliging and forgiving. Ineffective co-operative negotiators will come across as intelligent, dignified and self-controlled, but they may not be able to skilfully explore their counterpart's position or share the kind of information the counterpart needs in order to make a decision to settle the case. Potentially negative aspects of the co-operative negotiator's characteristics are passive-aggressive or victim behaviours.

Characteristics of the aggressive negotiator: The traits of effective aggressive negotiators include being dominating and forceful, as well as using strategic timing and an analysis of the sequence of events to advance their position. The aggressive negotiator is not interested in the needs of others. He or she will put forward an unrealistic and rigid opening position which may or may not include

---

[9]   Gerald R. William, "Style and Effectiveness in Negotiation" in L. Hall, *Negotiations: Strategies for Mutual Gain* (Newberry Park, CA: Sage, 1993), pp. 156-69.

overt or covert threats. Revealing information gradually and strategically, the aggressive negotiator is willing to "push the envelope" with regard to the facts in order to advance his or her case in the most optimal light.

The ineffective aggressive negotiator may exhibit irritating and quarrelsome traits. His or her behaviour may be overtly hostile and bullying in nature. This negotiator is generally unprepared on legal facts, may use bluffs, and will issue "take it or leave it" ultimatums. Often an unreasonable opening demand is made, and insufficient information is exchanged to allow the negotiation counterpart to make a decision about settling the case. The ineffective aggressive negotiator may also be demanding or argumentative and may come across as egotistical and arrogant. He or she is disinterested in the needs of others and intolerant of others' points of view.

Traits shared by effective negotiators, whether co-operative or aggressive, include:

- scrupulous preparation;
- honest and ethical conduct;
- understanding of the courtesies and negotiation customs in the industry;
- perceptive and skilful reading of verbal and non-verbal cues;
- effective use of advocacy skills;
- realistic, reasonable and rational approach to negotiation;
- persuasive manner; and
- self-control.

Advocates can be effective using either a co-operative or an aggressive stance. The challenge is to examine one's negotiating style and to ascertain and modify the ineffective traits. At the same time, effective advocates assess the preferred negotiating style of their negotiation counterpart as part of their strategy.

(b) Negotiating Strategy

The term "strategy" has been identified as "the negotiator's planned and systematic attempt to move the negotiation process towards a resolution favourable to his [or her] client's interests".[10] A planned and systematic approach includes consideration of the available negotiation models as well as the preferred styles and traits of effective negotiators. Strategy also includes preparing one's client and one's case[11] and considering tactics, traps and pitfalls.

A tactic is a technique used to further one's position, manipulate the other party and/or stall for time. The following is a list of common tactics which the author has observed in insurance negotiation.

A checklist of negotiation strategies/tactics is found in Appendix 3.1 at the end of this chapter.

---

[10] J. Gifford, "A Context-Based Theory, Strategy, Selection and Legal Negotiation" (1985), 46 Ohio St. L.J. 41. See also pp. 32-3.
[11] See the discussion at pp. 33-7.

Unclear authority: This tactic refers to the situation where, in the midst of negotiation, one of the negotiators, having been presented with an offer, says: "Well, I'm going to have to take the offer to somebody higher." This is not an uncommon situation in insurance mediation. Where it changes from a technique into a negative tactic is where the negotiators have not disclosed that there are other players who must be consulted before the case can be settled or others who are not presently involved in the negotiation. This tactic can be a way of buying time if a truly new and innovative option has been introduced. However, it can also be perceived negatively if the negotiators have been less than candid about the possible need for such consultation.

The potential adverse impact from use of this tactic can be dealt with by discussing authority to settle at the beginning of the negotiation and by making it clear that particular kinds of offers may have to go to another level in the organization. Counsel or representatives of the individual insured and organizational insurers should clarify whether they have authority to bind or to complete an agreement on the spot. Consider the situation where a very junior counsel has been assigned to a case and is rapidly getting out of his or her depth. Such a counsel may use the technique of unclear authority to buy time and save face while pursuing a conversation with his or her senior partner prior to completing a deal. Sometimes, too, individual plaintiffs are uncomfortable about committing to a settlement until they have consulted with a trusted family member or some other personal or professional advisor.

Pressure tactics: A graphic illustration of a pressure tactic in the labour environment is the strike or walkout. In the insurance industry, pressure tactics include procedural or legal actions such as filing for summary judgment or bringing an excessively large negotiation team to the table. The "dream team" approach can be intimidating to the opposing negotiator, particularly if the size of the team is unexpected or the nature of the case does not warrant a team approach to representation. The author has seen this tactic used by counsel bringing an instructing claims manager, an insurance adjuster in training, and a law clerk to what was perceived by the other side to be a simple face-to-face negotiation to commence discussions and explore the issues. This activity was viewed as a show of strength and power and did not result in constructive dialogue. In actual fact, it resulted in further delay because the negotiation was cancelled so the other counsel could put together a complementary negotiation team.

Use of threats: A typical threat surrounding a settlement in insurance negotiations is the phrase "Take it or leave it". There is great risk in introducing ultimatums such as this because the result may be to close down effective discussion and present the negotiator as an aggressive, intimidating unco-operative player. Other kinds of threats include attacks such as "You violated the policy" or "Your client lied". Intimidation may be subtler, such as "If you refuse to discuss this settlement option, we will be pursuing a lawsuit and will certainly win at trial". The difficulty with these kinds of attacks and intimidation is that rarely is a negotiator able to guarantee that he or she can make good on the threats. Often the threats are empty and have no basis in reality. Threats may be effective in showing a very aggressive stance, but they are ineffective in facilitating constructive dialogue.

Alternating negotiators: A tactic which has been used in the author's experience is changing negotiators midway through the negotiation. Sometimes this is an inadvertent action where those responsible for a file become ill, are transferred or leave the company. However, in just as many cases, this action can be a deliberate tactic to change the dynamics of the negotiation. It can have a positive result if the previous negotiator was unable to engage his or her negotiation counterpart. A new negotiator with a different style may be able, in a face-saving way, to salvage the negotiation discussions and give the opposing negotiator an opportunity to restart the discussions. On the negative side, if a rapport has been built up between the two negotiators and suddenly there is a new negotiator in the room, this can delay discussions and may adversely impact the progress of the negotiation.

Physical or geographical tactics: In negotiations and bargaining sessions, advocates may be concerned about where the negotiation will take place. If it is to be a full meeting with the clients present, there may be a perception of advantage to those whose office hosts it. This can be avoided through the use of external facilities such as court reporting services and hotel meeting room facilities. The geographical location of a client or the location of counsel may become a power tactic. For example, if the insurance company is located in a major centre and the plaintiff is not, the individual plaintiff may feel overtly pressured to travel. Even when negotiations do occur in a mutually acceptable place, the author has observed at least one situation where the two parties met in a very attractive boardroom with refreshments, coffee, etc. on the premises of one of the clients, but when the other party asked for an opportunity to meet privately with his client, they were escorted to a tiny airless room with a heating problem. This lawyer and his client were asked to wait in this room for a significant period of time in anticipation of a response from the other side. Needless to say, the imposition of this physical space was not constructive and in fact resulted in opposing counsel getting up, packing his bags, and leaving before proposals had been exchanged. Due consideration does have to be given to the physical premises, including the availability of refreshments, temperature-controlled facilities, sufficient numbers of comfortable chairs, proper meeting tables, etc.

Good cop/bad cop: This well-known technique is commonly and effectively used in many insurance negotiations. It can involve the lawyer and the client taking on different aggressive and co-operative negotiation roles. An effective good cop/bad cop combination, or tag team, utilizes the effective traits of both aggressive and co-operative negotiators. This provides an opportunity for the negotiators to engage with the negotiation counterpart regardless of the counterpart's style or preference. Used constructively, this technique can build quite a bit of momentum while allowing each participant to maintain his or her own preferred style. However, it is sometimes negatively perceived as one negotiator "beating up" on the counterpart. Effective advocates should plan for the good cop/bad cop technique, be alert to potentially negative effects on the negotiation counterpart, and be prepared to revise strategies if the technique is not producing the desired response.

The non-negotiator: As previously described under preferred negotiation styles, there are individuals who prefer to avoid dealing with the dispute or otherwise entering into negotiations. This approach can also be used selectively as a tactic to stall a negotiation or to provide an opportunity to ascertain the opponent's position without necessarily disclosing any information. Those dealing with non-negotiators should ascertain whether it is in their best interests to force the non-negotiator into participating or to attempt to motivate effective dialogue in another way. A non-negotiator using a passive-aggressive style can be extremely effective in stalling or closing down negotiation discussions.

Broken record: The broken record technique involves using circular arguments and repetitive statements which inhibit the negotiation from moving forward. This tactic should be recognized and corrected in a positive way. Occasionally, individuals fall into a cyclical pattern without recognizing the detrimental effect on the negotiation and may need a gentle prod to get them back on track. At the same time, if the broken record technique is being used with intent, this may be a reason to call a halt to the negotiations, take a break, speak with one's client, and/or call the negotiation counterpart's tactic. Identification of the behaviour in a non-confrontational, constructive manner gives the counterpart an opportunity to either provide the information required in order to continue the negotiations or to end the session.

Stalling: This tactic involves one negotiator using any technique to slow the negotiation down or to perpetuate it indefinitely. When stalling techniques are recognized, it is useful to ask the negotiation counterpart why time seems to be an issue. Very often, calling the bluff on a particular tactic will correct the behaviour.

These are just a small range of examples of the types of tactics used by advocates in the context of insurance industry negotiation. It is important to recognize these behaviours as they arise in one's own team or in the negotiation counterpart. The effective advocate recognizes tactics and uses open and courteous communication skills to correct the behaviour before reacting aggressively.

(c) Negotiation traps

The strategic negotiator needs to recognize potential pitfalls which may occur in any given negotiation. One author has identified a number of negotiation traps.[12] Those applicable to insurance negotiation are listed and described as follows. A checklist is contained in Appendix 3.2.

[12] R.J. Lewicki *et al.*, *Think Before You Speak: A Complete Guide to Strategic Negotiation* (Toronto, Ont.: John Wiley & Sons Inc., 1992), pp. 144-50.

Irrational commitment: This refers to negotiators agreeing to something for an irrational reason. An example in insurance negotiations is where one advocate has a personal bias against the negotiation counterparts or there is a negative negotiation history between them. These negotiators may be looking for reasons to support their assumptions and may not listen fully to reasonable arguments supporting a different point of view. In a professional negligence file, an engineer who has a dispute with his or her insurer about the level of coverage for a particular error may have an expectation that the insurer will seek an apology from the alleged victim. The engineer's position may be "set in stone" because he or she believes that no error was made and the role of the insurer is to put forward the needs and concerns of the insured. One way to avoid this trap is to use an advisor to provide a reality check. Generally, consulting with someone who does not have a stake in the process or the relationship is best.

Belief in a fixed pie: Another pitfall in negotiation is the belief that the resources in the negotiation are fixed, *i.e.*, there is a finite amount to be divided among the parties in the conflict. There may be an assumption that the outcome is a "zero sum" when there actually are options to "expand the pie". A competitive approach perpetuates the belief that there is a limited result, whereas a collaborative approach at least explores the possibility of other options. In the previous example of a slip and fall in a municipality, the case, which was assumed to be a pure quantum determination for an injured ankle, ended up including some overtures to a municipal government to increase citizen involvement in the identification of trouble spots for the elderly during Canadian winters.

Anchoring: "Anchoring" refers to the individual position or goal that a negotiation party has when entering the negotiation. The negotiator uses the anchor to benchmark the progress of the negotiation and any resulting agreement. In the slip and fall example, the plaintiff was told by her neighbour that her sprained ankle injury was worth $25,000. As a result, she came to the negotiation with an incorrect, preconceived idea of the quantum of her damages. This remained the case despite repeated and consistent dialogue with her legal representative indicating that this number was unrealistic.

Studies have shown that anchors can flaw negotiations if they are carelessly chosen or chosen on the basis of convenience rather than relevance.[13] Anchoring affects opening negotiation positions, negotiation objectives, and "bottom lines". An understanding of one's own and the other party's anchor can indicate how the negotiation will progress. This is particularly important if the anchor is different from what arises in negotiation. Research has shown that it is difficult to adjust pre-negotiation anchors during a negotiation. If the initial anchoring is too unrealistic, mutual satisfaction may be impossible. Further, the careless choice of anchors can detrimentally affect a negotiation before it begins. The lesson for the

---

[13] Glen Whyte and J. Sebenius, "Anchoring: A Valuable Tool or Deadweight", Executive Summary published by the Program on Conflict Management and Negotiation Centre for International Studies, University of Toronto, in *Coming to Terms: Shaping Effective Negotiation and Dispute Resolution*, Vol. 1, No. 2, 1998.

reflective advocate is that anchors should be chosen appropriately and selectively and the possibility of an unrealistic anchor canvassed with the client prior to the negotiation. Successful negotiation is premised on the foundation of preparation and anticipation.

Framing: "Framing" refers to the perspective from which a negotiator sees and evaluates information. A common framing issue in the insurance context is the characterization of an offer by a defendant as "nuisance value". The sophisticated negotiator will understand that this means the negotiation counterparts see no legal merit in the plaintiff's case. However, for economic, organizational and business reasons, they will consider making an offer to "make the case go away". A less sophisticated client may take the characterization of "nuisance" personally. The kinds of frames used and the forum in which they are used can positively or negatively impact the way the parties view the issues. For example, one party may see the negotiation as being about compensation for a physical limitation the victim now suffers, while the other party may see it as a consideration of the liability of the organization. These are fundamentally different views of the situation and need to be discussed. Failure to address these assumptions may result in the parties feeling like they are talking past one another rather than to one another.

Information: The availability of accurate and relevant information is essential to any negotiation. However, the way information is presented may be a barrier. Some individuals have a preference for colourful, graphic presentations, while others prefer a written synopsis of the case law. Negotiators need to be aware of any expectations or demands which might be read into the way in which issues are communicated. The effective negotiator takes into consideration the different ways information can be presented and ensures that sufficient information is provided to the negotiation counterpart in order to facilitate further discussion. Likewise, if the negotiator is not receiving sufficient information, it is incumbent upon that person to request the information and to state his or her rationale.

Winner's curse: This phrase refers to the concept of an "easy win", whereby the negotiation resolves very quickly and one party starts to question whether they settled too fast. This is a psychological trap which may result in the parties believing they missed out on something because the settlement was achieved too readily. This is a common pitfall in insurance negotiations where parties who have not fulfilled all the negotiation "steps" perceived to be an industry standard feel betrayed. To avoid this pitfall, negotiators should be thoroughly familiar with the area under negotiation so that not only is the objective value of settling known, but the personal value to the negotiator or advocate, the client, and the opposing negotiator and client are at least canvassed. The winner's curse does not usually afflict experienced, strategic negotiators because they are aware of commonly accepted patterns of negotiation and have already assessed a range of possible outcomes.

Overconfidence: Especially in negotiations involving legal representatives and institutional clients, confidence is extremely important. However, overconfidence can become a trap. Overconfident negotiators may take an inappropriate stance or support an incorrect view. They may ignore a point of view or information from the other party which is key to a collaborative or expansive resolution. Negotiators should pay attention to their level of confidence and do some self-observation as to how they approach a file and the enthusiasm with which they put forward their position to the other side.

A tangential pitfall to overconfidence is the error of ignoring the ideas of others. This can often happen where there are very experienced negotiators interacting with more junior ones or where clients are not communicating effectively with their counsel. The author is aware of a number of situations where a representative perpetuated one view of the facts while the clients tried to interject and correct. This resulted in embarrassment to the negotiator because some basic questions and ideas had not been canvassed in advance of the negotiation. This can be avoided by considering not only the positions of one's own client and opposing clients, but also possible underlying motivations.

Predictions: Negotiators sometimes fall into the error of making predictions for the future based on inadequate information. A classic example is where one negotiator has had a difficult time negotiating with another negotiator or insurance company. There may be an assumption that all negotiations with this person or insurance company will be the same. It should be recognized, particularly in the case of large organizations, that many different negotiators with many different styles of negotiation will represent that organization.

"Prediction" also refers to unrealistic reliance on legal precedent. If one case supports a view and there are numerous cases that do not, negotiators need to be careful that they have fully considered both possibilities. While past experience is very important, negotiators should avoid basing their expectations for current and future negotiations wholly on past experience. They should learn from others and use strategic processes to select different approaches from the ones which have failed in the past.

Inaccurate assumptions: Negotiators should do their homework to ensure they know who the parties are on the other side and their style and approaches used. There may be assumptions made about what caused the situation to occur and the motivations of the parties. Assumptions should be based on accurate, specific information, and they should be verified. Effective negotiators keep an open mind in order to ensure that they modify their assumptions appropriately and as needed. Negotiators need to be aware of personal bias and stereotyping. It is valuable to double-check one's facts and sources and avoid making any premature assumptions.

Ignoring others: One negotiation pitfall is the tendency to ignore the ideas of others. Quite simply put, effective advocates ask for clarification and seek verification rather than relying on assumptions. They ask questions to ensure they understand everyone's needs and concerns. Also, the generation of creative options is ideally achieved through the participation of all. Just because the negotiation counterpart comes up with a given idea does not mean the idea should be dismissed out of hand. Expert negotiators watch for bias.

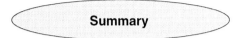

Summary

The following propositions have relevance to negotiations conducted in the context of insurance disputes.[14]

1. Negotiations rarely have to be win-lose, but neither are they likely to be win-win. Skilled negotiators tailor their tactics to the type of negotiation, seeking both to create value and to claim value by crafting creative deals which bridge differences.

2. Uncertainty and ambiguity are facts of life in negotiation. Skilled negotiators seek to learn and to shape perceptions through orchestrated actions taken at and away from the negotiating table.

3. Most negotiations involve existing or potential forces of conflict which could poison efforts to reach mutually beneficial agreements. Skilled negotiators are often called upon to mediate even as they negotiate, and intervention by outside parties is commonplace.

4. Interactions among negotiators are fundamentally chaotic, but there is order in the chaos. Skilled negotiators find opportunity in the fog of negotiation.

5. While negotiations occurring in diverse contexts may appear to be very different, they often have similar underlying structures. Structure shapes strategy, but skilled negotiators work to shape the structure.

6. Most negotiations are linked to other negotiations, past, present and future. Skilled negotiators advance their interests by forging and neutralizing linkages.

7. Negotiations are fragmented in time, and movement occurs in surges. Skilled negotiators channel the flow of the process and work to build momentum in promising directions.

8. Most important, negotiations take place between representatives of groups, and just as leaders are often called upon to negotiate, so are negotiators called upon to lead.

---

[14] Michael Watkins, "Negotiating in a Complex World", *Negotiation Journal*, Vol. 15, No. 3, July 1999.

9. Organizations are often represented by many negotiators, each of whom conducts many negotiations over time. Success in setting up organizational learning processes contributes to increased effectiveness, both individual and collective.

10. Negotiation skills can be learned, and they can be taught. Expert negotiators possess skills such as pattern recognition, mental simulation, process management and reflection-in-action, and these skills can be developed through carefully structured experience.

APPENDIX 3.1
CHECKLIST OF NEGOTIATION STRATEGIES/TACTICS[15]

☐ unclear authority
☐ pressure tactics
☐ use of threats
☐ alternating negotiators
☐ physical or geographical tactics
☐ good cop/bad cop
☐ the non-negotiator
☐ broken record
☐ stalling

APPENDIX 3.2
CHECKLIST OF NEGOTIATION TRAPS[16]

☐ irrational commitment
☐ belief in a fixed pie
☐ anchoring
☐ framing
☐ information
☐ winner's curse
☐ overconfidence
☐ predictions
☐ inaccurate assumptions
☐ ignoring others

---

[15] For a discussion of these points, see pp. 54-7.
[16] For a discussion of these points, see pp. 57-61.

Mediation

- Mediation is defined as "assisted negotiation".
- Mediation involves the use of a neutral third party, the mediator, who facilitates the exchange of information, uncovers interests, and assists the parties to explore options for mutual gain.
- The two main models of mediation used in the insurance context are evaluative mediation and facilitative or problem-solving mediation.
- The mediator can never impose a binding resolution on the parties regardless of the mediation model adopted.
- In evaluative mediation, the mediator provides the parties with a non-binding view or opinion of the merits of the case. This form of mediation can build upon positional or rights-based negotiation.
- Facilitative or problem-solving mediation encourages an interest-based approach and facilitates "principled" negotiation between the parties.
- Mediation in the insurance context can take place as a privately contracted process or as a mandatory process through court-connected programs or provincial insurance tribunals.
- Mediation builds on persuasive negotiation strategies.
- Effective advocates consider negotiation models, styles and tactics in preparing for mediation.

63

1. INTRODUCTION

Many insurance disputes are settled through direct negotiations or via the negotiation process used in mediation. Mediation has been shown to be particularly useful in resolving insurance disputes where there is an opportunity to structure a creative business solution.[1]

There are many models of mediation. Mediation in its simplest form consists of facilitated negotiation in which the mediator is an impartial third party who helps the parties in dispute reach a fair and mutually acceptable settlement by facilitating discussion and communication between them. While the mediator is never empowered to impose a settlement, the mediator's presence often alters the dynamics of the process and helps to define and shape the final settlement.

The mediation process, when conducted properly, can allow all parties to move away from legal concepts such as fault and blame towards the sharing of perceptions and experiences and a determination of each party's actual needs and interests. Some authors[2] have stated that such an outcome can often do more to truly resolve the problems which led to the dispute than any formal adjudicative hearing. In the context of the insurance industry, as well as many other types of commercial disputes, the mediation process encompasses both the legal principles, rights and obligations of the parties, and the underlying interests of the parties which may include personal, professional and economic concerns.

Mediation can result in a signed agreement or contract which prescribes the future behaviour or actions of the parties. This is often called a memorandum of understanding. Such an agreement has the force of a contract. When signed, it becomes binding on the parties.

2. PRELIMINARY CONSIDERATIONS

(a) When Should an Advocate Consider Using the Mediation Process?

When dealing with an insurance matter, advocates need to determine whether an institutional or a mandated form of mediation is required. For example, mediation involving insurance disputes may be mandated by an administrative tribunal such as the Insurance Commission of British Columbia or the Financial Services Commission of Ontario, or by a court-annexed ADR program such as

---

[1] CPR Institute for Dispute Resolution, "CPR Mediation Procedure" (Rev. 1998) [US/Canada], http://www.cpradr.org. To access this article, click on "Procedures & Clauses", then on "ADR Procedures US/Canada".

[2] Stephen B. Goldberg and Frank E.A. Sanders, "Fitting the Forum to the Fuss: A User-Friendly Guide to Selecting an ADR Procedure", *The Negotiation Journal*, Vol. 10, No. 1, January 1994.

Ontario's Mandatory Mediation Program. Considerations for mandated mediations are discussed later in the chapter. Mediation may also be mandated through a contractual obligation such as a dispute resolution clause in an insurance policy.[3]

Private mediation may be chosen in the insurance setting for the following reasons:

(1) The introduction of mediation brings a third party mediator who manages the negotiating process.

(2) Mediation adds structure to the negotiation process. As an impartial third party, the mediator will enforce the ground rules and ensure that discussions proceed fairly, objectively and in a productive fashion. Often the mere presence of a neutral third party in a negotiation/mediation process encourages constructive dialogue between the parties.

(3) Mediation promotes more effective communication. When discussions break down, the mediator can assist in facilitating communications between the parties by using active listening techniques such as open-ended questions, reframing and summarizing, refocusing the discussions, handling emotional outbursts, and being attentive to non-verbal communication.

(4) Mediation enables the parties to explore options and to create value in a safe environment, without fear of ridicule or exploitation.

(5) The third party in a mediation can provide a "reality check" when requested. This can include an independent assessment of the consequences of a particular course of action or even the likelihood of success of a particular strategy. In some insurance mediations, this assessment includes providing a non-binding view or opinion of the legal risks and liabilities associated with a particular set of facts.

(6) Depending on the mediator assigned or selected, the parties can expect the mediator to bring the following characteristics to the process: persistence, stamina, tenacity to bring the dispute to resolution or settlement, and optimism or an abiding belief that parties who want resolution can achieve it.

(b) Models of Mediation

A number of mediation models have been described in the conflict resolution literature over the past years. In the context of insurance litigation, two models need to be reviewed: evaluative mediation and facilitative or problem-solving mediation. Both these models have been used successfully to resolve insurance disputes.

In evaluative mediation, the mediator, who is chosen to assist the disputants in achieving a mutually acceptable result, evaluates the relative strengths and weaknesses of each party's legal claim. In this model, the mediator offers advice or an opinion on how the dispute is likely to be resolved should it proceed to

---

[3] See Chapter 6.

court or to arbitration. Once the evaluation is provided, the parties may be more inclined to accept a settlement consistent with the mediator's view.

In facilitative or problem-solving mediation, the mediator assists the parties to solve their dispute by improving communication between them and by searching for creative solutions which will advance the interests of both parties. He or she may assist the parties in reaching an agreement by acting as a referee and by directing the parties so that all have an opportunity to participate and to interact fully with each other. The mediator's primary role is to help the parties focus on the problem rather than on each other. Problem-solving strategies which may be employed include brainstorming, single text mediation, and other dialoguing techniques.

Readers should note that the two different models of mediation described here are consistent with the two types of negotiation models described in Chapter 3.[4] As with the negotiation process, effective advocates should be prepared to adapt to the use of different mediation models in the interests of furthering their case.

The evaluative and facilitative mediation models are often categorized as either "rights-based" or "interest-based" approaches. While this classification may be relevant for theoretical purposes, it is the author's experience that a combination of these two approaches is often used in the insurance context. For example, an evaluative style mediator may ask specific, direct questions or act as "devil's advocate" to ensure that the legal rules and precedents are considered in discussing the case. However, he or she may also use brainstorming or other kinds of interest-based techniques to ensure that a full range of settlement options is considered. Thus it is suggested that it may not be useful in practical terms to continue to compare and contrast the two models. A more useful framework might be to consider that the "rights" of the parties are one of the "interests" which must be considered in the mediation process.

(c) Agreements to Mediate

The following are the components which are generally included in agreements to mediate. A checklist of these components is included in Appendix 4.1 at the end of this chapter. In addition, a copy of a private mediation agreement is included in Appendix 4.2. The components of an agreement to mediate are:

Scheduled date of mediation: This section of the agreement should indicate the date, time and location of the mediation.

Parties: This section uses a court style of cause or title of proceeding. It is important for ensuring that all parties to the mediation are listed.

Name of the mediator: It is important to indicate the name of the mediator, especially if the parties have agreed to a particular person and the contract is with a firm with multiple mediators.

---

[4] See pp. 44-7 for a description of these two negotiation models.

Terms of mediation: This section sets out a description of the mediation process. An example of such a clause could be:

A mediation is a voluntary and informal settlement process by which the parties try to reach a solution that is responsive to their joint needs. Participation in this process is not intended to alter their existing rights and responsibilities unless they expressly agree to do so.

Role of the mediator: This clause describes and clarifies the role of the mediator. For example:

The mediator is a facilitator only, is not providing legal advice, legal representation or any other form of professional advice or representation, and is not representing any party. The mediator's role is to assist the parties to negotiate a voluntary settlement of the issues if this is possible.

Authority to settle: For clarity, the parties should agree in advance that their mediation representatives have binding settlement authority:

The parties will send to the mediation representatives with full, unqualified authority to settle, and they understand that the mediation may result in a settlement agreement which contains binding legal obligations enforceable in a court of law.

Mediation format: The parties should understand the mediation format to be used:

The parties will discuss the matter with the mediator individually or together, in person or by telephone, with a view to achieving settlement.

Drafting a memorandum of settlement: This clause is intended to expedite further proceedings and to clarify options regarding settlement:

If the matter cannot be settled voluntarily and if the parties agree, a memorandum listing areas of agreement or disagreement may be prepared by the mediator to facilitate future attempts at settlement.

Disclosure: A hallmark of successful mediation is the sharing of relevant information. The following clause deals with disclosure in the mediation:

Throughout the mediation, the parties agree to disclose material facts, information and documents to each other and to the mediator, and they will conduct themselves in good faith.

Without prejudice provision: Mediation is an extension of "without prejudice" settlement negotiations:

Statements made by any person, documents produced, and any other forms of communication in the mediation are off the record and shall not be subject to disclosure through discovery or any other process, nor are they admissible into evidence in any context for any purpose, including impeaching credibility.

Statement of issues: For efficiency purposes, the parties should clarify and share their understanding of the issues in dispute:

> The parties will deliver to the mediator and exchange with each other, not less than five (5) business days before the start of the meeting, a concise statement of the issues and the problem as they see them.

Stay of legal proceedings: It is important to the success of the mediation that the parties commit to negotiate. This commitment ensures good faith participation in the mediation:

> No party will, while the mediation is in progress, initiate or take any fresh steps in any legal, administrative or arbitration proceedings related to the issues.

Non-compellability of the mediator as a witness: This clause articulates the general understanding that the mediator is not compellable as a witness in a court or an administrative hearing to disclose what occurred during mediation:

> No party will, either during or after the mediation, call the mediator as a witness for any purpose whatsoever. No party will seek access to any documents prepared for or delivered to the mediator in connection with the mediation, including any records or notes of the mediator.

Confidentiality: Confidentiality in mediation is integral to the process. It is therefore critical that confidentiality be confirmed in the mediation agreement. A comprehensive clause setting out expectations and exceptions is set out in the following way:

> Except for what is stated in the rest of the mediation agreement, the mediation is a confidential process, and the parties agree to keep all communications and information forming part of this mediation in confidence. The only exception to this is disclosure for the purposes of enforcing any settlement agreement reached. The mediator will not voluntarily disclose to anyone who is not a party to the mediation anything said or done or any materials submitted to the mediator except:
> (a) to any person such as a professional advisor who is designated or retained by any party, as deemed appropriate or necessary by the mediator;
> (b) for research or educational purposes, on an anonymous basis;
> (c) where ordered to do so by judicial authority or where required to do so by law; and
> (d) where the information suggests an actual or potential threat to human life and/or safety.

Independent legal advice: The mediator's role as an impartial third party is paramount in any mediation:

> The parties are responsible for obtaining their own independent professional advice, including legal advice or representation if desired. The mediator does not provide same. The mediator has no duty to assert or protect the rights of any party, to raise any issue not raised by the parties themselves, or to determine who should participate in the mediation. The mediator has no duty to ensure the enforceability or validity of any agreement reached. The mediator will not be liable in any way, save for his or her wilful default.

Issues: The agreement to mediate will often include a clause which sets out a summary of the issues in dispute between the parties. It should be noted, however, that these issues may be revised and/or eliminated during the course of the mediation.

Cost of the mediation: In general, agreements to mediate set out a schedule of the mediation fees and indicate that the parties shall each bear their own legal expenses if any. Specifics around the fee schedule may include the mediator's hourly rate and an estimate of the number of hours expected to be needed for preparation and for participation in the mediation session(s). There is usually a statement that the estimated fee will not be exceeded without the prior written consent of the parties and a provision dealing with various expenses and disbursements including the costs of photocopies, facsimiles, mileage and venue. A cancellation fee is also stipulated to provide for the payment of fees should the mediation be cancelled. A typical cancellation provision will read as follows:

> Cancellation with notice of over three (3) working days prior to the scheduled mediation is subject to half the estimated fees. If the mediation is cancelled for any reason within the three (3) days prior, the full amount is payable.

Signing individually: Very often, a mediation agreement will provide a provision indicating that each party may sign a separate copy of the agreement which, when signed and delivered, shall be an original copy even though not signed by the other parties. All such separately signed copies shall together constitute evidence of consent by all the parties to be bound by the agreement. This is a purely practical provision, enabling the agreement to be signed and executed by each party prior to the formal mediation session.

Consent to mediation agreement: This clause indicates that each of the parties has read the agreement and agrees to proceed with the mediation on the terms contained in the agreement. It is the usual practice for a representative of each party, being either a person with signing authority or counsel for the party, to sign the agreement. Not all dispute resolution practitioners require the execution of a mediation agreement prior to commencing a mediation. However, it is the view of the author that best practices would require the signing of some sort of undertaking to ensure that the parties understand the nature of the mediation intervention and the terms and payment schedule of the dispute resolution practitioner.

3. THE MEDIATION PROCESS

(a) Generic Stages of Mediation

The actual stages of a mediation may vary depending on the preferences and style of the mediator and the disputants, the degree to which positions may have hardened during the progression of the dispute, and the complexity of the issues. In the insurance context, the mediation process commonly follows five general steps:

(1) pre-mediation considerations;
(2) introductions and opening statements;
(3) exchanging information and uncovering interests;
(4) generating options;
(5) reaching and documenting an agreement; and
(6) post-mediation considerations.

(i) *Pre-Mediation Considerations*

Many of the pre-mediation considerations such as agreeing on the selection of a mediator, outlining the terms, conditions and economic costs of the mediator, etc. are discussed in depth in Chapter 2, "Preparing for ADR". First the parties consider the suitability of mediation for their particular file. Mediation has become one of the most popular ADR choices of parties seeking a non-binding form of dispute resolution. Authors such as Stephen B. Goldberg and Frank E.A. Sanders have developed an analytical model to encourage parties to articulate their objectives and to apprise the likelihood that ADR processes will overcome the impediments to settlement. In one commentary by Goldberg and Sanders,[5] mediation is referred to as the "presumptive choice", recognizing that in most cases, analysis leads to the conclusion that mediation is indeed the most appropriate procedure. It should be reiterated, however, that the parties in a non-mandated or non-statutory context may have to persuade the other side to use mediation. In the insurance context, on the other hand, the use of mediation has become an industry practice, and many organizations automatically refer cases to mediation at particular points in the litigation process.

Having elected to proceed to mediation, the parties should consider who will attend the mediation as representatives, who are the appropriate parties to the mediation, the level of disclosure they would like to provide, and optimally, when the mediation should occur (pre-lawsuit, pre-discovery, post-discovery, etc.).

---

[5] Stephen B. Goldberg and Frank E.A. Sanders, *op cit.*, footnote 2.

(ii) *Introductions and Opening Statements*

The mediator opens the first session by setting out ground rules, outlining his or her expectations, and describing the role of the third party in managing the mediation process. The parties are encouraged to make opening statements which set out an abbreviated version of the facts and legal issues. These opening statements may be provided by legal counsel and/or by the client. Very often there is a "tag team" approach where the representative and the client work together to present the facts or alternate making statements about what they hope to accomplish in the mediation session.

(iii) *Exchanging Information and Uncovering Interests*

This is an extremely important stage of the mediation process. It provides an opportunity for the parties to ensure that all those at the table are operating on the basis of similar information or at least a mutual understanding of which facts are acknowledged by all and which issues are in dispute. New information is usually presented and/or documents disclosed at this time. Written mediation briefs exchanged prior to the mediation proper are often built upon.[6] The interests of the parties are canvassed and uncovered, particularly in a facilitative model. The mediator usually asks open-ended questions to clarify the facts, ascertain any business or professional needs of the parties, and validate any personal or economic motivators. This portion of the mediation is often conducted by alternating joint sessions and individual meetings or caucuses between the parties and the mediator.

(iv) *Generating Options*

Ideas and suggestions for resolving the conflict will arise throughout the course of the mediation. The parties may present a "wish list" in their opening statements, and there may be ideas presented by counsel or parties as they discuss their understanding of the case. The mediator will track these options in notes or on a flip chart or white board so that the parties can consider them at a later time. The option generation portion of the mediation is not necessarily a discrete stage, but may be integrated into some of the other stages. Very often, a list of options is discussed and used as a baseline for the parties in preparing proposals for reaching a resolution.

(v) *Reaching and Documenting an Agreement*

The parties, once they have had their full discussion and feel they have enough information to make an informed decision about trying to resolve the case, will try to reach a resolution in a number of ways. They may, for example, use the proposal/counter-proposal method. With this method, one party makes a proposal to the other. The other party seeks clarification and then retires with

---

[6]   See pp. 37-8 for a discussion on preparing an ADR brief.

counsel to contemplate a response or counter-proposal. Settlement offers can be presented in face-to-face meetings by counsel or can be put forth through the use of "shuttle diplomacy" via the mediator. Another method for seeking to reach resolution involves the parties taking the package of options which has been shared and going through it, ranking the options in order of high and low priority. This method can be blended with the proposal/counter-proposal method, with the parties fashioning their offers from a comprehensive list of options. If the mediator has offered an evaluation of the case or has been requested to do so by the parties, this can also affect reaching an agreement.

Once agreement is reached, the parties generally document their agreement, either in principle or comprehensively, in the form of a memorandum of settlement or minutes of understanding. These agreements may be drafted by counsel for the parties, and/or the mediator may take direction from the parties and draft an agreement to be signed on the spot. Mediators with legal backgrounds may be hesitant to participate in drafting the terms of settlement based upon concern that this activity could be construed as providing legal advice. Generally, this comes down to mediator style and party preference.

(vi) *Post-Mediation Considerations*

Implementation of the agreement is a primary consideration post mediation. Sometimes, if the case has not been settled at mediation, there are undertakings to share particular documents or to set up dates for examinations for discovery. The post-mediation considerations are very often prescribed in the mediation itself and, if there are issues or process concerns, it is advisable for advocates to raise those during the joint session.

(b) Characteristics of Mediation

(i) *Without Prejudice*

Mediations have been recognized as part of settlement discussions and thus are "without prejudice" to any further rights of the parties to legal proceedings. In other words, communication arising out of settlement discussions should not be used in evidence at a later time in another proceeding or forum. This stipulation is often included as a term of agreement in the mediation.

(ii) *Confidentiality*

A hallmark of mediation is the fact that it is a confidential and private process. There are two aspects to confidentiality in mediation. First, the mediator has an obligation to hold the information that comes to him or her during the mediation in confidence. Secondly, the parties are obliged to hold as confidential any exchanges made to each other during mediation sessions. Confidentiality is extremely important and is often the primary reason why parties wish to pursue this process as opposed to an open court process.

There are some exceptions to the principle of confidentiality. Most private mediation agreements set these out in writing. For example, the following clause is an excerpt from the agreement to mediate which is included in Appendix 4.2 at the end of this chapter:

> The mediator will not voluntarily disclose to anyone who is not a party to the mediation anything said or done or any materials submitted to the mediator except:
>
> (a) to any person such as a professional advisor who is designated or retained by any party, as deemed appropriate or necessary by the mediator;
> (b) for research or educational purposes, on an anonymous basis;
> (c) where ordered to do so by a judicial authority or where required to do so by law;
> (d) where the information suggests an actual or potential threat to human life and/or safety.

Even in situations where the parties have not, in advance of the mediation sessions, signed an agreement containing confidentiality provisions, it is expected, based on past experience in Canada and the United States, that the without prejudice and confidential aspects of the mediation process would be enforced in a court of law.

(iii) *Authority to Settle*

Another significant feature of the mediation process is the expectation that those who attend the mediation have the authority to make a decision should the mediation reach a stage where full and final settlement may be attained. The parties should give careful consideration to the authority to settle issue and ask the question: Who needs to be present at the mediation session for the purposes of achieving a final resolution? Authority to settle is important if the mediation process is to be relevant and in order to ensure efficiency in finalizing any agreement. If a potential agreement is reached and an outside absent party has final authority, this can upset the balance of power in a mediation. It has also been ruled that such a practice is unacceptable to parties wishing to pursue settlement discussions in good faith.[7]

While it is advisable and desirable to have parties and/or representatives with full settlement authority present at the mediation, advocates should be aware that there are different types of authority which may have bearing on a particular dispute. These types of authority have been characterized as:

- legal authority;
- advisory authority;

---

[7] *Magalhaes v. Lusitania Portuguese Recreation Club* (1999), 91 A.C.W.S. (3d) 728 (Ont. S.C.J.).

- conditional authority; and
- de facto authority.[8]

Legal authority refers to the competence and capacity of individuals to make decisions and may have an impact where a party is an artificial entity such as a corporation.

Advisory authority has been described as the ability to verify data, financial or legal assumptions. An example would be input from an accounting advisor or from an engineer in a construction-related dispute.

Conditional authority refers to the situation in an insurance dispute where, for example, settlement requires approval from outside sources such as a reinsurer.

De facto authority refers to individuals who may not have legal, advisory or conditional authority, but who could in reality obstruct the implementation of a settlement if not present at the mediation sessions or consulted.

(iv) Voluntary

Private mediations are voluntary because the parties take part by choice. However, even in situations where mediation is mandated by either the courts or an administrative tribunal such as the Financial Services Commission of Ontario, full participation in the mediation is still voluntary. The parties may argue that showing up at the session fulfils their attendance requirement, although, in the author's view, this behaviour does not constitute good faith participation. As well, the mediator has no power to impose an outcome or settlement in either a private or a mandated mediation. It should be noted that, while the mediation process is voluntary, any agreement arising out of it, such as a memorandum of understanding, is binding on the parties and will contain legal obligations enforceable by law.

(c) Mediation Processes

There are different formats for conducting a mediation session. These include:

(a) a joint meeting of all the parties;
(b) individual meetings or caucuses;
(c) telephone conference calls; and
(d) exchange of documents.

The mediation may be conducted entirely in the format of a joint session, where the mediator acts as chairperson, enforcing ground rules and directing dialogue. Generally all parties are present who have been identified as being key to the case. These include legal representatives and clients with authority to settle.

---

[8] Richard J. Weiler, "Authority to Settle and Mediation", *Alternative Dispute Resolution Practice Manual* (Toronto: CCH Canada Ltd., 1996), ¶50,050.

A mediation may also be conducted entirely by way of caucusing or through private meetings between the mediator and the individual parties. Caucuses may take place during the mediation proper or may be used as part of the input and preparation stage of mediation. For example, in a large insurance dispute where there are multiple defendants, it may be strategic to have the mediator meet initially with the defendants as a group in order to assist them in working out their relationships with one another prior to meeting together with the plaintiff. These meetings allow the mediator to explore issues and concerns with the parties without necessarily sharing those issues and concerns with the other side.

Advocates should ask the mediator to describe his or her practice regarding information obtained in a caucus. There are two approaches generally adopted by mediators in this regard. In the first approach, any information obtained in caucus is not shared with the other side unless the mediator is expressly authorized to do so. Conversely, the mediator may advise the parties that he or she will assume that any information divulged in caucus can be shared with the other side unless expressly instructed not to do so. Individual practices and styles do vary greatly in this regard, so it is useful to verify this with the individual mediator.

Use of telephone conference calls to conduct mediations is increasing, particularly in administrative tribunals where the economic and administrative costs associated with having all parties meet face-to-face in one location are becoming prohibitive. In the case of mediations conducted at the Financial Services Commission of Ontario, the mediator, in consultation with the parties, determines whether to conduct the mediation by way of telephone conference or in a face-to-face meeting. If a telephone conference is selected, the mediator conferences with the parties, providing his or her opening statement and asking the parties to describe their objectives and what they want to achieve from the mediation. After the mediator identifies the issues in dispute, he or she can continue the mediation with all the parties on the telephone or decide to caucus with the parties. If the second alternative is chosen, the mediator hangs up the phone and calls each of the parties back to conduct the caucus.

One of the disadvantages of telephone mediation is that important visual cues such as body language cannot be captured. Also, where the credibility of a party is an issue, which is a common occurrence in insurance cases, telephone mediation is not the preferred choice. Finally, where the issues in dispute are numerous and complex, and/or there is a lot of documentation in the file, teleconferencing is not appropriate.

The exchange of documents is not so much a mediation format as an influence on the format. Some parties use exchange of documents as a condition precedent to mediation or to commence negotiations by including a written offer in the mediation brief. Exchange of documents is important in both face-to-face and telephone mediation because it lays the groundwork for discussions and shows good faith through the sharing of relevant information before the mediation begins. Failure to share information dilutes rapport and can become a barrier to meaningful discussion.

(d) Anatomy of a Mediation

Following are two case studies used to illustrate the different ways mediations can progress. In the first scenario, both the plaintiff and the defendant are insurers disputing a subrogated claim. In the second, the plaintiff is an individual with limited experience in the legal system and the defendant is an insurance company. In these examples, the activities of the advocates and their clients are described in the context of typical mediation procedural steps, including pre-mediation negotiations. Commentary on the progress of each scenario is included to provide an analysis of the strategies employed.

CASE SCENARIO 1 – BARN BURNING

Background: The property of Farmer Brown was damaged by the actions of three children who broke into his barn and played with matches. Apparently, acetone and other flammables were stored in the barn, and the building burned to the ground. The children escaped with no injuries. Farmer Brown's insurer, ABC Fire & Casualty Co. ("ABC"), conducted an investigation and paid the insured the amount of $75,000. Further investigation by the police and the fire marshall raised the question as to whether the flammables were properly stored in such an old wooden barn. Apparently, the barn was over 50 years old and made of aged, dry barn board. A newer farm building was located about a kilometre away, so the old barn was a secondary building. The investigation also revealed that the children were two brothers, aged 11 and 13 at the time of the incident.

ABC commenced legal action against the parents of the two children, alleging that the parents were responsible for the damage caused by their children's unsupervised activities. Happy Homeowners Insurance responded to the subrogated claim as the parents' insurer.

> [Commentary: A subrogated claim is a claim where one creditor is substituted for another. In this case, the farmer's insurance company was going after the parents of the children who caused the loss. Another example which is typical in the insurance industry is where an unemployment insurance or a provincial health insurance plan must be paid back out of the proceeds from an out-of-court settlement.]

ABC took the position that the parents were totally liable for the actions of their offspring and therefore liable for the full amount paid to Farmer Brown plus costs. Happy Homeowners Insurance denied liability and stated that, in any event, Farmer Brown was guilty of contributory negligence.

Early negotiation discussions: Several telephone conversations regarding the file took place between the adjusters after the statement of claim was issued. At that point in time, ABC had offered to reduce the claim by 15% or $11,250, and to accept the amount of $63,750. Costs and interest were not discussed. By way of counter-offer, the adjuster for Happy Homeowners proposed paying a

$5,000 nuisance value in return for a full waiver and discontinuation of the lawsuit. Happy Homeowners further proposed that each party cover its own costs. At this point, negotiations stalled.

Assignment of counsel: The dispute was then handed over to counsel for Happy Homeowners and ABC. The statement of claim and statement of defence were on file. Legal counsel for the various companies sent letters to each other or picked up the phone and proposed mediation as a way of resolving the dispute. Counsel exchanged names of mediators and mediation dates. Eventually, agreement was reached regarding a mediator and a date for the mediation. The mediator sent out his standard agreement to mediate [similar to the one included in Appendix 4.2 at the end of this chapter]. At this point in time, examinations for discovery had not been made. Counsel agreed that the goal of the mediation was to try to reach some kind of settlement.

At the mediation: At the first joint meeting of the mediation, the mediator introduced himself and set out some ground rules for the conduct of the mediation. These ground rules included asking the parties to be courteous and respectful in their communications, to not interrupt each other, and to try to avoid reverting to "cross-examination" mode. The mediator verified that the meeting was confidential in accordance with the agreement to mediate and asked whether the parties in the room had authority to settle. The mediator had reviewed the parties' briefs ahead of time. He asked the parties who would like to go first in terms of an opening and setting out the facts of the case. As is often the case, counsel for the plaintiff started. The opening statements in this particular scenario were made either by counsel alone or by counsel in conjunction with the person attending as decision-maker for the particular insurance company. As part of their opening statement, counsel set out the relevant facts of the case and their "wish list" in terms of settling the file.

> [Commentary: The dialogue in a mediation like this would be somewhat different than in a mediation where the plaintiff was not experienced in the legal system. It could be expected in this scenario that the parties were both very sophisticated in negotiating and participating in mediation and that, if the insurance adjuster did not take an active role, this was because he had chosen not to for strategic purposes.]

Exchange of information and clarification of underlying interests: The parties asked some questions of each other, and the mediator asked open-ended questions to ensure that everyone understood exactly what had happened. The ages and circumstances of the children, as well as the investigative reports of the fire marshall and the police, were the topics next discussed.

> [Commentary: While it could be anticipated that there were probably underlying interests in settling this file, particularly given that the case law around this particular subrogated claim was quite ambiguous, this aspect was not discussed openly. Whether or not this is done will vary, depending on the

style of the mediator and of counsel. Nevertheless, mediation advocates should be aware of that subtext. The subtext of professional competitiveness should also be considered as an informing factor in selecting a negotiation/ mediation strategy. It is worthwhile to know what kind of relationship there is between the two lawyers on the file. Do they typically appear across the table from each other? Very often, lawyers who do a lot of defence work for insurers are not comfortable in the plaintiff role. This is a situation where the mediator can be of assistance in directing and moving the conversation along in order to address that discomfort. Likewise, the competitive nature of the business may come out in the relationship between the two adjusters. It is useful to ascertain whether these individuals are the two adjusters who conducted the initial negotiation or whether they are different representatives of the insurance companies who have been selected to come to the mediation. Once again, the previous negotiating relationship of the parties is going to be important in determining how a mediation proceeds.]

Individual meetings: Given the type of insurance claim at hand, the mediator asked to meet with each of the parties within an hour or an hour and a half of the commencement of the mediation. During these individual meetings, the mediator elicited additional information from the parties, including whether there was any ongoing relationship between the companies.

[Commentary: Amalgamations, mergers and strategic alliances between cor-porations have become one factor influencing how mediations progress as well as the terms of settlement. It may be useful to understand whether there are any economic or business interests in terms of closing the file at a particular time or avoiding the creation of a precedent. These underlying business interests will usually be canvassed by the mediator within the privacy of a caucus in order to allow the parties an opportunity to strategically disclose information as they wish.]

During the individual meetings, the parties gave the mediator information they did not want to share with the other side. For example, ABC had paid out too much money under the policy, which provided for market value of the barn, not replacement value. This being the case, it was reasoned that Happy Homeowners' counsel and representative would be disinclined to reimburse the full $75,000.

[Commentary: It is not inconceivable that Happy Homeowners would have done some research and understood that the market value of similar structures in this particular area would have been in the range of $25,000 to $40,000. There may also have been a view that no one should obtain an economic gain or windfall from the case.[9] On the other hand, research may have shown that the property was worth more without the barn and that Farmer Brown was

---

[9] See p. 17 for a discussion of the jackpot syndrome.

actually better off after the loss since he would have had to spend $25,000 to have the barn removed. These are examples of information that the parties may choose to disclose to the mediator in caucus in order to assist in moving the mediation forward, or the parties may choose to share the information with each other directly in the exchange of information portion of the mediation. If there is particular information that the mediator feels the other side must have in order to make an informed decision, including conducting a cost-benefit analysis on settling the file, he or she may encourage the party to share it directly with the other side, or the mediator may ask permission to take that information to the other party. For example, ABC's initial goal in filing the subrogated claim may have been to send the strong message that individuals, including children, will be held accountable for their actions, and that insurance companies are not deep pockets designed to cover other people's negligent parenting. It may be that the adjuster who paid out the large amount in error was no longer with ABC and that ABC would like to recover at least part of the erroneous payout. The mediator may seek permission to share any or all of this kind of information.]

Generating options: The mediator tracked various settlement options in his notes and on a white board. The options identified at this point were:

- pursuing the case to trial;
- discontinuing the action without costs;
- Happy Homeowners paying ABC compensation, including damages, prejudgment interest, legal costs and disbursements;
- Happy Homeowners including something in its homeowners policies stating the types of losses covered.

In view of the financial nature of the case, the breadth of settlement options was limited. Given that negotiations on these settlement options had already occurred, the mediator encouraged the parties to make another proposal to try to settle the file. He suggested that the parties craft their proposal, keeping in mind that it takes a minimum of several offers and counter-offers to resolve any given file. He also drew on the information provided in the openings, *i.e.*, the initial offers to settle at $63,750 and $5,000 respectively. However, since these amounts did not result in a settlement of the case prior to mediation, the parties seriously considered whether they could move beyond those amounts to a settlement. Happy Homeowners made a proposal to ABC, offering to compensate the casualty insurer for 50% of the damages, assessed at $25,000, plus 15% or $1,875 for legal costs and $625 for interest, the total settlement being $15,000. This offer was conditional on the exchange of mutual releases and discontinuing the action without costs. The mediator encouraged Happy Homeowners to make this proposal directly to ABC and to include a rationale as to why this amount was being offered. ABC then met with its client to discuss responding to the offer. ABC responded by stating that it accepted that the payout was in excess of what was permitted under the terms of the contract. However, it further stated that its assessment of the damages was $40,000, and its assessment of Farmer Brown's contributory negligence was 15%. Therefore, ABC offered to take $34,000 plus $2,000 for costs and interest, the total being $36,000. At that point, the parties met privately to consider their options. The parties had moved from being $58,750 apart to $21,000 apart, still a fairly significant difference. The mediator encouraged each of the parties to put another set of proposals on the table in order to move them closer to agreement.

[Commentary: At some point in the mediation process, the adjusters may ask to speak to each other alone to try to work out an agreement. In a case such as this, the professional respect which each of the adjusters has for the other could play a pivotal role. In a case where the plaintiff is an unsophisticated newcomer to the legal system, the lawyers might be the ones who ask to speak to each other privately. It is up to the mediator to provide a neutral space for that and to assist in whatever way possible to facilitate continuing dialogue between the parties.]

Reaching and documenting an agreement: The mediator presented some suggestions for settlement. The parties could split the difference and settle for $25,500 total. In the alternative, they could re-examine their analysis and perhaps adjust their perception of contributory negligence or the amount of damages. For example, the parties could use ABC's assessment of $40,000 and apply Happy Homeowners' reduction of 50%, which would result in an offer of $20,000 plus 15% costs, plus interest, or the parties could present another round of proposals. The parties finally settled for an all-inclusive sum of $26,000.

[Commentary: Once the parties agree on a settlement amount, they will probably draft minutes of settlement. Sometimes one or the other of the parties has a set of standard releases. It is important to prepare the agreement on the spot in order to save time, ensure that the parties leave with a mutual understanding of how and when the money is going to be paid and to whom, and canvass how the case will be withdrawn from court.]

Summary and analysis: This scenario is a classic example of a file where both of the parties are relatively equal in their background and bargaining power. While the file was mediated using a facilitative or problem-solving approach, there did not appear to be many interests at play in the ultimate settlement. The interests which occurred in the real life file were generally concentrated around the relationship between the two adjusters and the relationship of the lawyers to their respective insurers. In similar files, the author has observed situations where the law firm representing a particular insurer had just been told that his or her retainer would not continue after the file, leaving the lawyer disgruntled and not at all comfortable with participating in the mediation. There was a definite lack of co-operation between counsel and insurer in those files. Keeping this in mind, advocates should actively consider and solicit information with regard to the business or organizational needs of the insurer. The topic of reserves and in-house expectations regarding precedent setting are not generally discussed openly with individual plaintiffs. However, where the decision-makers in the room have similar qualifications and levels of responsibility, the parties may feel more comfortable speaking about these topics. Also, if it appears that legal counsel is not moving quickly on the case and the insurance adjusters or decision-makers have become "bored" with the process, the parties may seek a face-to-face meeting on their own to try to close the deal. Mediation, in such a situation, would have given the parties an opportunity to do cost-benefit and legal risk analyses of the file and to show each other their seriousness about pursuing resolution. Very often, files of this nature are settled at the negotiation stage. However, a mediation can be of assistance in setting up a neutral forum to achieve settlement. Also, where the person responsible for the file has changed midstream, mediation is a face-saving way of allowing a representative decision-maker of the insurer to ask to meet and discuss the file with the opposing decision-maker in a neutral setting.

CASE SCENARIO 2 – SLIP AND FALL

Background: Ms. Smith, an 80-year-old resident of a small town municipality in Saskatchewan, slipped and fell on a major street corner and sustained a broken ankle. As a result of the injury, Ms. Smith was hospitalized and underwent an open reduction of the ankle. The legal position of the plaintiff was that the defendant, Small Town Saskatchewan, was negligent in failing to keep the said street clear and safe. She pleaded that she had sustained severe damage and was entitled to full, general and punitive damages. The defendant, Small Town Saskatchewan, took the position that the plaintiff was entirely at fault for her slip and fall. The town stated that there was no evidence presented that the municipality was liable for this loss, and it argued that there was no legal merit to the notion that a municipality is responsible for indemnifying every person who has an unforeseen incident in a Canadian winter. In the alternative, if such liability did exist, the municipality pleaded that it had fulfilled its responsibility to keep the street free and clear of ice. Furthermore, the municipality held that the plaintiff was contributorily negligent in causing her misfortune.

Pre-mediation considerations: In this particular file, there were no pre-mediation settlement discussions. The statement of claim and statement of defence were filed, and the case was sent to mandatory mediation under the civil rules of procedure. Prior to the mediation, counsel spoke to each other on the phone with regard to the issues and agreed that the following issues were in dispute:

(1) Was the defendant liable for negligence in failing to keep the said street free and clear of ice?
(2) To what extent was the plaintiff contributorily responsible for the damages incurred?

(3) What, if any, was the amount of damages payable to the plaintiff?

The mediation brief included Ms. Smith's medical file, which outlined the nature of the complaint, the physician's notes, and the fact that she had gone to the operating room for an open reduction of a fractured ankle. The medical record also included additional comments that, on admission, the patient had been quite hypothermic and agitated and had stated that she had been waiting in the cold for an ambulance for approximately 30 minutes.

Introductions and opening: The assigned mediator opened the mediation by introducing the parties and ascertaining their comfort level in being called by their first names. He outlined some general ground rules, including courtesy and lack of interruption, and he articulated that it was the mediator's role to enforce the ground rules and keep the process moving. The mediator indicated that the parties were welcome to have a break or to meet privately with the mediator or with their own client or their counsel. The respective counsel outlined the facts of their individual case and indicated that they were there to talk about settlement.

> [Commentary: In a case like this, counsel may ask their client to participate in the opening statement, partly as a sympathy factor and partly to provide a first-hand explanation of the events.]

The plaintiff participated directly by describing what occurred during the slip and fall and the circumstances surrounding her injury. The defendant representative of the municipality, which was self-insured, described the actions taken by the municipality to keep the street free and clear of ice, the procedures for doing so, and the activities surrounding the arrival of the ambulance.

Exchange of information and clarification of issues: Once the opening statements were completed, the mediator invited the parties to ask questions. The plaintiff was asked very specific questions by the defendant's counsel in order to ascertain exactly what had happened. The questions included inquiries about the plaintiff's footwear, her medical condition prior to the accident, any economic out-of-pocket losses, the exact location of the accident, and the sequence of events with regard to the slip and fall. Plaintiff's counsel asked the municipality specifics about the procedures used to keep the street clear. At this point, the parties provided each other with additional documents such as medical records, copies of policies and procedures, and copies of reports by the town foreman investigating the incident.

> [Commentary: As in the first example, underlying interests might not be directly canvassed. However, the mediator would ask questions, if this has not been done by the parties, as to the impact of the incident on the plaintiff's life and if the plaintiff has any particular concerns he or she wishes to share. Likewise, the defendant would be questioned about organizational and business concerns with regard to indemnifying every person who slips and falls in a Canadian winter. Counsel would likely give a brief overview of the

state of the law with regard to municipal slip and fall accidents and comment on the level of liability which might be proven in court.]

Generating options: During a private meeting with the plaintiff, the mediator ascertained that she had obtained an opinion from her neighbour over the back fence regarding an amount for settlement.

> [Commentary: This is a typical example of the concept of anchoring described in Chapter 3.[10] It may be that counsel on a particular case may not be someone who routinely litigates slip and fall cases and may not be comfortable in providing his or her client with cost-benefit and risk analyses regarding the possibilities of success in court.]

At this point, the mediator, during a caucus, led the plaintiff and her counsel through a cost-benefit analysis, including discussing how long it would take to get to trial, the approximate cost, what someone's best day in court would look like, and what the worst day in court might look like. Discussion ensued, directed by the mediator, with regard to being realistic and not making assumptions about either the "win the lottery day in court" and/or the "burn in hell day in court". Following this discussion, the mediator tried to ascertain what the motivating factors were behind the plaintiff's pursuit of a resolution. He also tried to find out what negotiations had occurred prior to the mediation and how he could best assist the parties.

In a private caucus with the defendant, the mediator discussed some of the municipality's needs and concerns with regard to indemnifying everyone who walks on a Canadian street in the winter. The mediator made the following statement: "In the opening, you mentioned that you could not indemnify everyone who walks on a Canadian street in winter. Could you tell me a little more about that?" The mediator also asked if there were other factors to be considered such as the ratification of any settlement by the town council, impact on the town's public relations, and the presence of other cases which might influence the settlement of this particular file. Counsel for the municipality indicated to the mediator that they were prepared to make a small payment in the approximate amount of $5,000 as a "nuisance" value.

> [Commentary: It is ideal when this kind of information is shared in private caucus because an injured plaintiff might find the characterization of "nuisance" to be insulting and an attack on his or her credibility.]

The municipality's representative and counsel also indicated concern with being perceived as "deep pockets" and providing "win the lottery" awards to people in situations which did not warrant such compensation.

Having ascertained that the parties were willing to at least consider making proposals to each other, the mediator encouraged them to make a proposal on the

---

[10] See pp. 58-9.

basis that if at least one party made a proposal, the other one would respond. The plaintiff proposed that damages be assessed at $25,000 and offered 70 cents on the dollar to settle the same day, inclusive of costs and interest.

[Commentary: This kind of offer could be made through the mediator via "shuttle diplomacy" or face-to-face. The offer would include signing mutual releases and discontinuation of the core proceeding without costs.]

The municipality, in private consultation with the mediator, indicated that it was very uncomfortable with submitting a counter-proposal at a low level because it would be insulting to the plaintiff. At this point, the mediator went back to the plaintiff and asked again what she really wanted out of the mediation. The plaintiff replied that she really wanted a trip to Florida. The mediator probed this assertion and asked why a trip to Florida was something for which the municipality should pay. Upon further discussion, it was discovered that the plaintiff was an active volunteer in the community and had received an award for excellence which included a trip to Florida for a conference recognizing the volunteers' efforts. Because the plaintiff had fallen and broken her ankle, she had been unable to attend, and the trip was not something that could be transferred to another date. As a consequence, the plaintiff felt very strongly that she had been "duped" out of a hard-earned trip which she could not duplicate on her fixed pension. The mediator asked permission to share this information with the municipality and, on consent, did so. The municipality pondered this new information and decided that it could make an offer of a particular amount of money to pay for a trip to Florida, along with a nominal amount for legal fees and interest. It felt far more comfortable about making an offer at a smaller level, and the plaintiff felt comfortable accepting something below her assumed number coming into the mediation since the offer and the rationale addressed her primary concern. Her lawyer was able to support her decision because the case law was ambiguous and her original number unrealistic. In this way, both parties were able to mutually meet their need of being put back into the position they would have been in had the slip and fall not happened, but at the same time, the municipality did not have to pay out an exorbitant amount of money for a case which was low-risk based on the case law. On a personal level, the municipal counsel and in-house insurance representative were satisfied that they had not been part of implementing any "windfall" settlement.

4. BEYOND BASICS

(a) Selecting a Mediation Strategy

One of the goals of mediation is to provide an opportunity to reach a mutually acceptable settlement option within a shorter time-frame than would be possible by proceeding to court. There may be other objectives to be achieved from the process, such as reviewing the facts in more detail, obtaining a view of the other side's case, and, for some, conducting a "mini-discovery". Working closely with their clients, mediation advocates should ascertain at the outset what objectives the client wishes to achieve during mediation. These objectives will inform the selection of strategy to be adopted in the mediation.

Advocates attempt to persuade the other side of the merits of their client's case through their behaviour, emotions aroused in the other parties, and/or logical and intellectual argument. Persuasion through effective speaking or behaviour lends credibility to the speaker and engages the opposing parties. To be persuasive, advocates must consider tone of voice, type of language, knowledge, speaking style, listening ability and behaviour (*e.g.*, enthusiasm, optimism, etc.). The skill of active listening is pivotal for effective advocacy in mediation. Advocates actively listen to the participants by rephrasing, maintaining eye contact, feeding content back to the speaker, and asking questions when appropriate. Persuasion through non-verbal communication may include the way the parties are dressed, their stance at the table, how they look at the other parties, and the level of interest expressed non-verbally. For example, in a file where one of the parties sat drumming the table with his fingers and staring out the window, the opposing party did not feel that this party was really listening to what was going on. Inadvertent fidgeting is common and, once recognized, is a simple habit to correct.

Even as negotiators can choose from among different negotiation styles,[11] the mediation advocate can choose to use competing behaviours, accommodating techniques or compromise, collaboration, and/or avoiding strategies. The mediator should pay attention to his or her own approach to dealing with conflict and to the style used by others.

Caucusing can be used strategically to help identify tactics adopted by the other side, engage the mediator as a messenger, and clarify information without necessarily sharing it fully with the other side. Caucuses are frequently used in the insurance industry to allow counsel and client an opportunity to regroup and review the progress of the mediation.

Other procedural tactics may include controlling the meeting times or places and prescribing activities which may occur outside the mediation. One procedural tactic commonly being used is postponement or adjournment of the mediation while limited discovery takes place or expert advice or reports are gathered. Threatening to withdraw from the mediation process is a further procedural tactic, although threats to withdraw are risky in that the opposing party can call the bluff, thereby terminating future dialogue.

(b) Using the Mediator Effectively

Advocates should ensure that they make the best use of the mediator and the mediation process.

Reasonable first offers can be made through the mediator. It is not recommended that the party's bottom line be disclosed at the outset of mediation.

---

[11] See pp. 51-3 for a discussion of the various negotiation styles.

Rather, advocates should listen to the mediator and watch for clues about the other side's strategy and bottom line. Advocates need to ensure that information is transmitted gradually throughout the process. They should not feel compelled to share all information up front, particularly information relating to their client's underlying needs and concerns. When caucusing with the mediator, advocates should advise the mediator what information is confidential and should not be shared with the other parties. Any new proposals should be supported with sound reasons. Before making or accepting an offer, advocates should ensure they have the authority to settle.

The advocate's message should be consistent with his or her tactics. If an advocate exhibits a very hard line, he or she may have to soften that stance at some point if the real intent is to settle.

Creative problem-solving techniques have been used in many mediations in conjunction with a positional or evaluative model. The general and specific needs of the parties can influence the menu of options from which a proposal/counter-proposal process draws ideas. Prior to mediation, effective advocates should experiment with potential solution patterns and discuss these with their client.

In a personal injury or wrongful death case, consideration may be given to formulating a structured settlement. This type of settlement may be recommended where the plaintiff is a minor or an individual otherwise incapable of managing a substantial cash payout. Additional considerations regarding the use of a structured settlement include who will design the settlement and the type and amount of the settlement.

The mediator can be used to achieve closure of the process. In the case of impasse, it could be suggested that the mediator present a proposal as his or her own idea. Sometimes the mediator can be directed to explore settlement options without commitment. There may be a suggestion that the parties split the difference or that a structured settlement or instalment payment method be put in place. Some mediation counsel have advocated the use of an apology as part of the mediation settlement. Use of apology should be clearly thought out and, if made, be sincere and credible. Offering to exchange an apology for an amount of money is often rejected. The most effective use of apology is offering a sincere acknowledgment of the damages or injury incurred by the plaintiff without admitting liability.

(c) Strategic Opening Statements

The parties' opening statements should be succinct and relevant to settlement discussions, introducing the advocate and the advocate's client. Some advocates have the client tell the story using a narrative style. Advocates should listen to the client, make notes of any admissions, ask pertinent follow-up questions, and make concluding remarks. Many advocates refer to documents in their opening statements, particularly documents which have been provided prior to the mediation to both the mediator and the opposing party. Audio-visual aids have been used as part of an opening and will be discussed later in this chapter.[12]

---

[12] See pp. 89-90.

The opening statement should include a commitment to the process. Advocates should communicate their intention to listen carefully and to engage in serious discussion.

If applicable, some advocates acknowledge their client's fault or error at this stage. If the client has made a mistake in the course of the dispute, *e.g.*, failing to respond to a letter or using foul language, some advocates take this opportunity to acknowledge that and to apologize, or they may have the client make the apology personally. Acknowledgment of other circumstances such as lapse of time, inconvenience, etc., also shows good faith.

If there are agreed items, these should be mentioned during the opening statement. Advocates may wish to refer to some of their client's interests, including personal, professional and business considerations. It is important during the opening statement to outline the important issues from the client's perspective or to have the client share this personally. Advocates should share the strengths of their client's position, using objective criteria. Some advocates highlight relevant cases, legislation, contracts and expert reports during the opening.

(d) Use of Experts in the Mediation Process

Since mediation advocacy has become increasingly sophisticated, the use of expert evidence in the process has become more prevalent.

(i) *Effect of Industry Practice and Regulation*

In the insurance context and the personal injury field, it is common practice to obtain reports from experts such as medical and rehabilitation specialists and actuaries. A structured settlement expert or broker may be retained to assist the parties in examining a multiplicity of options in order to maximize a cash settlement. In the construction industry, the use of expert evidence includes first-hand testimony as well as comprehensive reports from engineers, architects, and specialists in particular construction industry practices.

In many ADR processes, the use of experts and expert evidence has become institutionalized. During mediation and arbitration before insurance tribunals such as the Insurance Commission of British Columbia or the Financial Services Commission of Ontario, expert reports are routinely used to substantiate claims.

(ii) *At What Stage of Mediation Can an Expert Be Used?*

Experts can be used prior, during and post mediation. In the pre-mediation phase, experts may be retained to analyze specific portions of the case and to provide a report. Experts are sometimes used to develop a negotiation strategy in order to ensure that the mediation goes forward on the best possible foot. In one case involving multiple defendants within a specific industry, an expert was retained specifically to assist the corporation in setting up the mediation steps. This promoted efficiency as well as providing a strategy to maximize the possible outcomes. Experts are also used to gather data prior to intervention, to establish industry benchmarks, and to analyze evidence.

It is not unusual for an expert witness to accompany the parties at the mediation as a resource person. In a case involving fiber optic technology, for instance, experts provided an opportunity to get answers to substantive questions and to clarify some difficult technical points. When bringing an expert to a mediation meeting, it is wise to notify the mediator as well as the other parties and their solicitors of this intention. This is a common courtesy, it provides the other parties with an opportunity to bring their own expert if necessary, and it prevents the perception of ambush at the mediation. Without prior notice, an honest attempt to provide clarity through the use of an expert could be construed as one-upmanship. This often negates counsel's ability to have a constructive dialogue about settlement.

While experts attend the mediation as members of the team for one party or another, their actual participation requires the consent of the other parties. It is helpful to set out the expert's role in advance in order to pre-empt any perceptions that his or her role is to evaluate the opposing parties' evidence or credibility. An example of this is where one party brings along a communications expert who has the ability to read non-verbal behaviour. Rather than building rapport and trust, this can be off-putting to mediation participants if they are not notified of the expertise. When bringing experts to mediation, advocates should be prepared to ask the expert to sit in a separate room or to attend the meeting as needed if there is opposition to having him or her participate in the entire mediation.

The use of intervenors with expert knowledge was discussed in Chapter 1.[13] When using intervenors with specialized substantive knowledge, the parties should clarify in advance with the intervenor what use they wish him or her to make of that knowledge. If the parties wish the intervenor to use his or her knowledge to ask appropriate questions, that is very different from using it to evaluate the case. Intervenors should not evaluate cases unless the parties intend them to do so. Consider the situation where one mediator gave unsolicited opinions about the merits of the case, particularly the credibility of the technical evidence, when the parties did not wish this information to be shared. Evaluative views given without consent not only undermine the credibility of the intervenor, but could seriously thwart settlement discussions.

Experts have also been retained at the conclusion of a mediation as part of the agreed resolution of the parties or as part of further procedural steps to reach resolution. Experts have been used to provide a mutual expert report evaluating the substantive technical aspects of a case. Parties should consider whether such reports should be binding or non-binding. The mediator can be of assistance in setting out the terms and conditions for these kinds of evaluations. Sometimes one or more of the parties require that a claim be verified or costed out. This may include the provision of medical records to prove a disability, actuarial reports to cost out long-term care costs, or an engineering report to set out damages to a structure during construction.

---

[13] See pp. 9 and 24.

5. PRACTICE TIPS

(a) Use of Demonstrative Evidence in Mediation

While mediation is an adjunct to the legal process, evidence may or may not be produced during the various mediation meetings. Sometimes demonstrative evidence such as maps, blueprints and photographs can have a powerful impact. Demonstrative evidence needs to be used selectively and should not dominate the mediation. Advocates should consider whether it informs or whether its intention is to intimidate and overwhelm. While intimidation may seem like a useful negotiation strategy, it does not always result in constructive dialogue leading to resolution. As part of the preparation for mediation, advocates should focus on the evidence with the most impact and take care to introduce such evidence in their opening statements. Documentary backup for graphic types of presentations is helpful. Some counsel have taken to using videotaped or Power Point presentations to demonstrate their theory of a case or to demonstrate problems with a structural design.

One of the most common types of demonstrative evidence used in mediation is videotaped surveillance. This is often used by insurance companies or corporations to show that a plaintiff is malingering or that damages are not as extensive as they are claimed to be. Video surveillance is most powerful when it rebuts evidence a claimant has made on discoveries or information provided to his or her doctor.

Most video surveillance has less impact than what is expected by those showing it. It has been used at mediation in a number of ways. One method is to show the tape as a prelude to the mediation. In one case, the surveillance, taken through a thatched hedge, showed the plaintiff raking the yard and pushing a wheelbarrow. However, instead of causing the plaintiff and plaintiff's counsel to renege and drop the case, this surveillance video had the opposite effect. Counsel and plaintiff became so incensed and inflamed that they packed up and left the mediation, and a date was set for trial. There was some question as to whether the identification of the plaintiff was going to be accepted at trial and whether the three-minute clip of the plaintiff allegedly pushing around the wheelbarrow was going to assist the defendant. In another mediation, this time mid-way through the joint meeting, videotaped surveillance was introduced and the plaintiff and his lawyer were given an opportunity to go and view the tape in private in a separate room. The plaintiff came back with his lawyer smiling and proudly told the room that the tape was that of his twin brother. In yet another case with a different result, videotaped surveillance was presented during the mediation, and counsel for the plaintiff returned and told the rest of the disputants that they would be going home and that he would be giving the defence lawyer a call in a couple of days to talk about dropping the case. In this particular instance, surveillance had been presented so that the plaintiff could save some face.

Those introducing videotaped surveillance evidence in mediation should be prepared for any number of reactions from the plaintiff and his or her counsel.

Surveillance video should be carefully considered for its utility prior to being used in a session. It should be edited to be sure it does not take up too much time, and there should be an openness by the parties to new information and explanations. Last but not least, videotaped surveillance should be considered in the context of the full case, including damages and claims.

(b) Use of Experts in Mediation

Experts in the mediation context can assist in determining what assumptions should be relied on and what may be reasonable in trying to reach a resolution. Likewise, if experts are going to be retained post-mediation, either jointly or separately, the mediation session can be used to negotiate the assumptions the experts will ultimately use in their report. Then the caucus room provides an opportunity for experts to discuss and narrow the range of outcomes based on either common assumptions or a narrower range of assumptions as the parties desire. Sometimes the parties use experts who opine as to what is the most likely explanation or outcome for the situation in conflict. Use of experts in the mediation session can dramatically reduce the scope of disagreement and reduce the likelihood of positional bargaining. This can considerably narrow the range or window of opportunity for negotiating a mutually agreeable settlement.

The informed use of experts can enhance and expedite every phase of the mediation process. In considering the use of a substantive expert, the parties should clarify the role of the expert prior to any joint meetings. They should consider whether the expert is to be a partisan witness or be available as a resource. If the expert is to be a mutual resource, has full consent for this been obtained from all the parties? Last but not least, the cost of experts can be quite a significant factor. A cost-benefit analysis should be conducted when assessing the utility of having an expert attend the mediation as a participant.

6. BARRIERS TO RESOLUTION – WHEN MEDIATION FAILS

Not all mediations result in a mutual agreement. There are a number of reasons why these assisted types of negotiations fail. One author has identified the following barriers:[14]

- strategic barriers;
- problems with the principal or agent;
- cognitive barriers; and
- reactive devaluation of compromise and concessions.

Strategic barriers include the disputants' behaviour and lack of commitment to "expand the pie". In the case of insurance mediation where the solution is very often distributive in nature, the parties often miss the potential benefits of

---

[14] Robert H. Mnookin, "Why Negotiations Fail: An Explanation of Barriers to the Resolution of Conflict", *The Ohio State Journal on Dispute Resolution*, Vol. 8, No. 2, 1993.

collaborative problem-solving approaches which would allow them to maximize the options for settlement. In order to create value, it is critically important that options be considered in light of both parties' underlying interests and preferences. This was illustrated in the second case scenario given in this chapter where the interests of the victim of a slip and fall were to be put back to where they would have been absent the fall, that is, she received her missed trip to Florida. Failure to consider this underlying interest could have resulted in a stalemate and/or an inability to settle until later in the legal process. Lack of full disclosure can also be a barrier to settlement, particularly if disclosure by one side is unreciprocated by the other side. In the first case scenario, where the two insurance companies were in a dispute about a subrogated claim, the lack of symmetrical disclosure about the actual amount of money paid out and the error which had been committed in paying replacement value rather than market value could have resulted in an unnecessary deadlock. This might have resulted in failure to discover options leading the parties to settlement.

Problems with the principal or agent can also be a barrier to a mediated settlement because the incentives for the advocate, whether a lawyer, employer, employee or officer, negotiating on behalf of the party may not be compatible with the interests of the principal. Insurance adjusters may have professional needs to settle a file in a particular way, which may or may not move the situation towards expedient resolution. In the slip and fall case previously discussed, counsel for the plaintiff may have had professional concerns given that they did not typically work in the personal injury field. This lack of confidence and certainty about the patterns of negotiation and types of settlement might have prevented the settlement from going forward if counsel had asserted options which were incorrect or unprofessional.

Cognitive barriers include difficulties in understanding information and processing the risks and uncertainties involved in any given case. Full disclosure may not be sufficient if it is not done in a way which is understandable by all the parties. In the insurance field, there is often a lot of "lingo" which may preclude the parties from fully engaging. Cognitive barriers also refer to individual preferences or values such as loss aversion. Parties in mediation who have locked themselves in or "anchored" their position based on predefined values or assumptions may not be open to the possibilities presented in a mediation or negotiation session. This particular barrier can be addressed by reframing the dispute away from the win-loss characterization in order to engage the parties and give them a "face-to-face" way of resolving the problem.

Reactive devaluation of compromises and concessions is an example of a psychological barrier. With regard to the dynamics of the negotiation process, negotiators draw inferences from their interactions which may or may not be correct. If one party offers to settle a case for a particular amount which is very close to what the other party thought was a good settlement, rather than reaching agreement on the first round, the receiving party may say, "We weren't asking for enough" or "What does the other party know that we don't know".[15] There are assumptions about who goes first and the seriousness of offers which may devalue even the most good-faith proposal. This is sometimes characterized as the "negotiation dance" and is equally applicable to mediation. As previously described in the case studies, the author has noted that it most often takes a minimum of several offers or proposals in order to settle a case: a proposal, a counter-proposal, and a couple of massages. This addresses reactive devaluation and allows the parties time to get used to the idea of accepting the range of options offered. Part of mediation is psychological, and that is to ensure that the parties are satisfied that the outcome meets their mutual needs.

7. MANDATORY MEDIATION

Mandatory mediation programs exist under some rules of civil procedure and some administrative tribunals. For advocates in the insurance context, these programs fall into two main areas: tribunals governing motor vehicle accident benefits and court-annexed programs. Privately contracted mediation advocates in these mandatory programs should consider the following questions. The questions are also included as a checklist in Appendix 4.3 at the end of this chapter.

Who administers the program? Advocates should verify who administers the mandated program. They need to be clear where to direct their questions, complaints or concerns regarding the program.

What types of cases are covered? The type of case varies widely between jurisdictions. For example, the Ontario Mandatory Mediation Program is integrated with case management so that only case-managed files are covered by the rule.

What are the obligations of counsel with regard to filing documents and the time limits for arranging mediation? Time frames and the exchange of documents are usually prescribed by the particular program. Effective advocates are aware of these and include them in their internal case management processes.

Who mediates? Do the parties get to choose? Who schedules the mediation? In some programs, mediation is provided by staff dispute resolution officers who are assigned cases by the administrators. Under the Ontario Mandatory Mediation Program, the parties have the option of selecting a mediator from a roster of mediators compiled by the local Mediation Committee, or they may select a mediator who is not on the list if all the parties agree.[16] In either case, the mediator must comply with Rule 24.1 of the *Rules of Civil Procedure.*[17] The Ontario Ministry of the Attorney General has prepared guidelines for selecting mediators and an application form for applicants, as well as a code of conduct for mediators

---

[15] See p. 59 for a discussion of "winner's curse".
[16] *Rules of Civil Procedure*, R.R.O. 1990, Reg. 194, subrule 24.1.08(2). See Appendix 4.4 for the full text of Rule 24.1.
[17] *Ibid.*, subrule 24.1.08(3).

which incorporates the Canadian Bar Association (Ontario) Model Code of Conduct.

Who pays for the mediation? Mandatory programs may provide mediators and meeting rooms at no charge, or the costs may be passed on to the parties. Sometimes the fees are prescribed by tariff. In either case, the parties are responsible for their own legal costs. Advocates should also consider whether any fees are payable if the mediation is cancelled.

What is the process for obtaining an exemption and/or extending the time limits? Some programs provide a process and criteria for obtaining an exemption. Likewise, an extension of time limits may be available under certain circumstances. The process for obtaining an extension may be as simple as filing a notice of consent of the parties or appearing before a master and presenting legal argument. Advocates should note any case law applicable to their circumstances.

What about disclosure and/or discovery of documents? Are there any rules about exchanging documents? It is common practice to exchange documents and briefs prior to mediation. Most mandated mediation programs have specific forms and requirements in this regard.

Who must attend the mediation? In addition to strategic considerations, advocates should consider that mandated mediation programs may have specific attendance requirements. The Ontario rule requires that the parties and, if they are represented, their lawyers must attend the mediation session unless the court orders otherwise.[18] Judicial determinations in this regard have affirmed this requirement.[19]

Is there a prescribed mediation format? Given the flexibility of the mediation process, advocates should be aware that some programs prescribe the format. For example, in the Ontario Mandatory Mediation Program, mediation is defined as follows: "In mediation, a neutral third party facilitates communication among the parties to a dispute, to assist them in reaching a mutually acceptable resolution."[20] It has been noted by some authors that this description does not confine the mediator or the parties to any one model of mediation.[21] Mediation at the Financial Services Commission of Ontario, for example, can be face to face, but it is more often conducted via telephone conference call.

Are there any repercussions for non-compliance? In an institutionalized setting such as a court or administrative tribunal, there may be consequences for non-compliance. Advocates should be aware of the situations which may give rise to such consequences.

---

[18] *Ibid.*, subrule 24.1.11(1).
[19] *Magalhaes v. Lusitania Portuguese Recreation Club* (1999), 91 A.C.W.S. (3d) 728 (Ont. S.C.J.).
[20] *Rules of Civil Procedure*, rule 24.1.02.
[21] Garry D. Watson and Paul M. Perell, "Rule 24.1 Mandatory Mediation" [unpublished]. Garry Watson is a professor at Osgoode Hall Law School, and Paul Perell is a partner at the law firm of Weir & Foulds in Toronto.

What about post-mediation responsibilities? Many programs require the filing of reports or evaluations by the mediator and/or the participants.

What is the role of counsel in a mandatory mediation process? The role of counsel in mandatory mediation is similar to the role of counsel in traditional litigation advocacy. Mediation advocates serve the best interests of their clients and assist and advise them in moving towards an appropriate result. As with other forms of litigation advocacy, counsel are in a position to fully analyze all the facts and issues relevant to the dispute and to assess the strengths and weaknesses of the case. Mediation is an opportunity for them to explore settlement options after giving the facts and risks due consideration. The roles of legal counsel may involve the following:

- educating the client prior to the mediation session about the mediation process and about the roles and responsibilities of the various participants;
- reviewing client goals and objectives with regard to the mediation and examining the strengths and weaknesses of the case.

It is contemplated that counsel will prepare some kind of mediation brief outlining the circumstances leading to the dispute, the history of the court proceedings and negotiations, and the documents relevant to constructive settlement discussions. Counsel should also prepare an opening statement setting out the facts, the case law, and the concerns and needs of the client. The opening may be made in conjunction with the client as part of the strategy. It is recommended that all counsel for the parties pick up the phone and speak to each other prior to the mediation in order to ensure that timely disclosure of documents occurs and to provide an opportunity to address pre-mediation concerns. Counsel should gain some understanding of the philosophy and models used by the mediator prior to the mediation session. If a full or partial settlement is achieved at mediation, counsel will play a key role in constructing a written agreement to be signed by all the parties.

Summary

Mediation is a tool to assist negotiation, to focus the problem, and to enable the parties to generate creative options which might not otherwise be canvassed. Mediation offers an opportunity for the parties to meet in a neutral, safe setting with prescribed ground rules and behavioural expectations. The parties can rely on the mediator to enforce these ground rules and to focus the discussions. Mediation advocates should recognize that the mediator is there to serve them and they should be used efficiently, effectively and strategically. Parties attending mediations should be prepared, and they should have planned who will discuss specific matters and considered the type of mediation solutions they might contemplate. Mediation can be an evaluative, positional process, or it can be conducted in a problem-solving, facilitative way. It is the author's experience that a good mediator will most often utilize multiple techniques and will change his or her techniques according to the needs of the parties. In preparing for mediation, the parties should consider their negotiation style and preferred approach. They should also review the roles of all the parties involved.

APPENDIX 4.1
LIST OF COMPONENTS GENERALLY INCLUDED IN AGREEMENTS TO MEDIATE[22]

- ☐ scheduled date of mediation
- ☐ parties
- ☐ name of the mediator
- ☐ terms of mediation
- ☐ role of the mediator
- ☐ authority to settle
- ☐ mediation format
- ☐ drafting a memorandum of settlement
- ☐ disclosure
- ☐ without prejudice provision
- ☐ statement of issues
- ☐ stay of legal proceedings
- ☐ non-compellability of the mediator as a witness
- ☐ confidentiality
- ☐ independent legal advice
- ☐ issues
- ☐ cost of the mediation
- ☐ signing individually
- ☐ consent to the mediation agreement

---

[22] For a discussion of these points, see pp. 66-70.

APPENDIX 4.2
SAMPLE AGREEMENT TO MEDIATE[23]

MEDIATED SOLUTIONS INCORPORATED

1802 - 415 Yonge Street
Toronto, Ontario, Canada M5B 2E7
(416) 408-1700

AGREEMENT TO MEDIATE

1. SCHEDULED DATE OF MEDIATION: Friday, May 5, 2000
(10:00 a.m. to 4:00 p.m.)

2. PARTIES:

agree to mediate certain differences through the services of Mediated Solutions Incorporated, 1802-415 Yonge Street, Toronto, Ontario M5B 2E7, (416) 408-1700, with Anne E. Grant, R.N., LL.B., LL.M. (ADR), C.Med. as mediator.

3. TERMS OF MEDIATION:

The parties agree to abide by the Terms of Mediation attached.

4. ISSUES:

The parties will deliver to the mediator and exchange with each other, not less than five (5) business days before the start of the meeting, a concise statement of the issues and the problem as they see them. The issues to be mediated as understood at this time are summarized as follows:

5. COSTS OF THE MEDIATION:

Unless otherwise arranged, the parties are jointly and severally responsible for the costs of the mediation. The fees are as set out in Schedule "A". The parties shall each bear their own legal expenses, if any.

6. SIGNING INDIVIDUALLY:

Each party may sign a separate copy of this agreement which, when so signed and delivered, shall be an original copy even though not signed by the other

---

[23] For a discussion regarding agreements to mediate, see pp. 66-70.

parties. All such separately signed copies shall together constitute evidence of all parties' consent to be bound by this agreement.

7. CONSENT TO THIS AGREEMENT:

Each of us has read this agreement and agrees to proceed with the mediation on the terms contained in it.

Party:_____   Party:_____

Date:_____   Date:_____

Mediated Solutions Incorporated

Per:_____

Date:_____

SCHEDULE "A"

FEE SCHEDULE

The full amount is due and payable five (5) working days prior to the scheduled mediation.

Mediator Fee:	$ per hour plus GST		$
Estimated Fees:	hours @ $	for mediation	$
	hours @ $	for preparation	$
		Plus GST	$
		TOTAL ESTIMATED FEES	$

Not to be exceeded without the prior consent of the parties

Estimated Expenses:	Photocopies @	$0.25 per page	$
	Facsimiles @	$0.25 per page	$
	Other @	$	$
	Mileage @	$0.38 per km	$
		Plus GST	$
		TOTAL ESTIMATED EXPENSES	$

TOTAL ESTIMATED FEES AND EXPENSES: $

Cancellations: Cancellation with notice of over five (5) working days prior to the scheduled mediation is subject to half the estimated fees. If the mediation is cancelled for any reason within the five (5) days prior, the full amount is payable.

TERMS OF MEDIATION

1.   Mediation is a voluntary and informal settlement process by which the parties try to reach a solution which is responsive to their joint needs. Their participation in the process is not intended to alter their existing rights and responsibilities unless they expressly agree to do so.

2.   The mediator is a facilitator only, is not providing legal advice, legal representation or any other form of professional advice or representation, and is not representing any party. The mediator's role is to assist the parties to negotiate a voluntary settlement of the issues if this is possible.

3.   The parties will send to the mediation representatives with full, unqualified authority to settle, and they understand that the mediation may result in a settlement agreement which contains binding legal obligations enforceable in a court of law.

4.   The parties will discuss the matter with the mediator individually or together, in person or by telephone, with a view to achieving settlement.

5.   If the matter cannot be settled voluntarily and if the parties agree, a memorandum listing areas of agreement or disagreement may be prepared by the mediator in order to facilitate future attempts at settlement.

6.   Throughout the mediation, the parties agree to disclose material facts, information and documents to each other and to the mediator, and they will conduct themselves in good faith.

7.   Statements made by any person, documents produced, and any other forms of communication in the mediation are off the record and shall not be subject to disclosure through discovery or any other process, nor are they admissible into evidence in any context for any purpose, including impeaching credibility.

8.   No party will, while the mediation is in progress, initiate or take any fresh steps in any legal, administrative or arbitration proceedings related to the issues.

9.   No party will, either during or after the mediation, call the mediator as a witness for any purpose whatsoever. No party will seek access to any documents prepared for or delivered to the mediator in connection with the mediation, including any records or notes of the mediator.

10.   Except for what is stated above, the mediation is a confidential process, and the parties agree to keep all communications and information forming part of this mediation in confidence. The only exception to this is disclosure for the purposes of enforcing any settlement agreement reached. The mediator will not voluntarily disclose to anyone who is not a party to the mediation anything said or done or any materials submitted to the mediator except:

(a) to any person such as a professional advisor who is designated or retained by any party, as deemed appropriate or necessary by the mediator;

(b) for research or educational purposes, on an anonymous basis;

(c) where ordered to do so by a judicial authority or where required to do so by law;

(d) where the information suggests an actual or potential threat to human life and/or safety.

11.   The parties are responsible for obtaining their own independent professional advice, including legal advice or representation if desired. The mediator does not provide same. The mediator has no duty to assert or protect the rights of any party, to raise any issue not raised by the parties themselves, or to determine who should participate in the mediation. The mediator has no duty to ensure the enforceability or validity of any agreement reached. The mediator will not be liable in any way, save for his or her wilful default.

April 24, 2000

Appendix 4.3
Generic Considerations When Participating in a Mandatory Mediation Process in Administrative Tribunals and the Courts[24]

In addition to the checklists contained in the Appendices at the end of Chapters 1 and 2, effective advocates should be aware of any rules or case law setting out obligations and limitations in the following areas:

☐   Who administers the program?

☐   What types of cases are covered?

☐   What are the obligations of counsel with regard to filing documents and the time limits for arranging mediation?

☐   Who mediates? Do the parties get to choose?

☐   Who schedules the mediation?

☐   Who pays for the mediation?

☐   What is the process for obtaining an exemption and/or extending time limits?

☐   What about disclosure and/or discovery of documents? Are there any rules about exchanging documents?

☐   Who must attend the mediation?

☐   Is there a prescribed mediation format?

☐   Are there any repercussions for non-compliance?

☐   What about post-mediation responsibilities?

☐   What is the role of counsel in a mandatory mediation process?

---

[24] For a discussion of this topic, see pp. 92-4.

APPENDIX 4.4
RULE 24.1 OF THE RULES OF CIVIL PROCEDURE – MANDATORY MEDIATION, INCLUDING THE APPLICABLE FORMS AND AMENDMENTS TO TARIFF A
As amended to O. Reg. 447/00

RULE 24.1 MANDATORY MEDIATION

PURPOSE

24.1.01 This Rule establishes a pilot project for mandatory mediation in case managed actions, in order to reduce cost and delay in litigation and facilitate the early and fair resolution of disputes.

NATURE OF MEDIATION

24.1.02 In mediation, a neutral third party facilitates communication among the parties to a dispute, to assist them in reaching a mutually acceptable resolution.

DEFINITIONS

24.1.03 In rules 24.1.04 to 24.1.16,

"defence" means,

(a) a notice of defence (Form 77B);
(b) a notice of intent to defend,
(c) a statement of defence, and
(d) a notice of motion in response to an action, other than a motion challenging the court's jurisdiction;

"mediation co-ordinator" means the person designated under rule 24.1.06.

APPLICATION

Scope

24.1.04 (1) This Rule applies to actions that are,

(a) commenced in a county named in the Schedule to this subrule, on or after the date specified for that county in the Schedule; and
(b) governed by Rule 77 (Civil Case Management).

Schedule

County	Date
City of Toronto	January 4, 1999
Regional Municipality of Ottawa-Carleton	January 4, 1999

Exceptions, Certain Actions

(2) This Rule does not apply to:

1. An action under the *Substitute Decisions Act, 1992* or Part V of the *Succession Law Reform Act*.

2. An action that is commenced in the City of Toronto and governed by Rule 76 (Simplified Procedure).

3. An action in relation to a matter that was the subject of a mediation under section 258.6 of the *Insurance Act*, if the mediation was conducted less than a year before the delivery of the first defence in the action.

Proceedings Against the Crown Act

(3) In an action to which the *Proceedings Against the Crown Act* applies, if the notice required by section 7 of that Act has not been served, the Crown in right of Ontario is entitled to participate in mediation under this Rule but is not required to do so.

EXEMPTION FROM MEDIATION

24.1.05 The court may make an order on a party's motion exempting the action from this Rule.

MEDIATION CO-ORDINATOR

24.1.06 The Attorney General or his or her delegate may designate a person as mediation co-ordinator for a county named in the Schedule to subrule 24.1.04(1), to be responsible for the administration of mediation in the county under this Rule.

LOCAL MEDIATION COMMITTEES

Establishment

24.1.07 (1) There shall be a local mediation committee in each county named in the Schedule to subrule 24.1.04(1).

Membership

(2) The members of each committee shall be appointed by the Attorney General so as to represent lawyers, mediators, the general public and persons employed in the administration of the courts.

(3) The Chief Justice of the Ontario Court [Superior Court of Justice] shall appoint a judge to be a member of each committee.

Functions

(4) Each committee shall,

(a) compile and keep current a list of mediators for the purposes of subrule 24.1.08(1), in accordance with guidelines approved by the Attorney General;

(b) monitor the performance of the mediators named in the list;

(c) receive and respond to complaints about mediators named in the list.

MEDIATORS

List of Mediators

24.1.08 (1) The mediation co-ordinator for a county shall maintain a list of mediators for the county, as compiled and kept current by the local mediation committee.

(2) A mediation under this Rule shall be conducted by,

(a) a person chosen by the agreement of the parties from the list for a county;

(b) a person assigned by the mediation co-ordinator under subrule 24.1.09(6) from the list for the county; or

(c) a person who is not named on a list, if the parties consent.

(3) Every person who conducts a mediation under subrule (2), whether named on the list or not, is required to comply with this Rule.

(4) Without limiting the generality of subrule (3), every person who conducts a mediation under subrule (2) shall comply with subrule 24.1.15(1) (mediator's report).

MEDIATION SESSION

Time Limit

24.1.09 (1) A mediation session shall take place within 90 days after the first defence has been filed, unless the court orders otherwise.

Extension or Abridgment of Time

(2) In considering whether to exercise the power conferred by subrule (1), the court shall take into account all the circumstances, including,

(a) the number of parties and the complexity of the issues in the action;

(b) whether a party intends to bring a motion under Rule 20 (Summary Judgment), Rule 21 (Determination of an Issue Before Trial) or Rule 22 (Special Case);

(c) whether the mediation will be more likely to succeed if it is postponed to allow the parties to acquire more information.

Postponement

(3) Despite subrule (1), in the case of an action on the standard track, the mediation session may be postponed for up to 60 days if the consent of the parties is filed with the mediation co-ordinator.

Selection of Mediator

(4) The parties shall choose a mediator under subrule 24.1.08(2).

(5) Within 30 days after the filing of the first defence, the plaintiff shall file with the mediation co-ordinator a notice (Form 24.1A) stating the mediator's name and the date of the mediation session.

Assignment of Mediator

(6) If the mediation co-ordinator does not, within the times provided, if any, receive an order under subrule (1), a consent under subrule (3), a notice under subrule (5), a mediator's report or a notice that the action has been settled, he or she shall immediately assign a mediator from the list.

(7) The assigned mediator shall immediately fix a date for the mediation session and shall, at least 20 days before that date, serve on every party a notice (Form 24.1B) stating the place, date and time of the session and advising that attendance is obligatory.

(8) The assigned mediator shall provide a copy of the notice to the mediation co-ordinator.

PROCEDURE BEFORE MEDIATION SESSION

Statement of Issues

24.1.10 (1) At least seven days before the mediation session, every party shall prepare a statement in Form 24.1C and provide a copy to every other party and to the mediator.

(2) The statement shall identify the factual and legal issues in dispute and briefly set out the position and interests of the party making the statement.

(3) The party making the statement shall attach to it any documents that the party considers of central importance in the action.

Copy of Pleadings

(4) The plaintiff shall include a copy of the pleadings with the copy of the statement that is provided to the mediator.

Non-Compliance

(5) If it is not practical to conduct a mediation session because a party fails to comply with subrule (1), the mediator shall cancel the session and immediately file with the mediation co-ordinator a certificate of non-compliance (Form 24.1D).

ATTENDANCE AT MEDIATION SESSION

Who is Required to Attend

24.1.11 (1) The parties, and their lawyers if the parties are represented, are required to attend the mediation session unless the court orders otherwise.

Authority to Settle

(2) A party who requires another person's approval before agreeing to a settlement shall, before the mediation session, arrange to have ready telephone access to the other person throughout the session, whether it takes place during or after regular business hours.

FAILURE TO ATTEND

Non-Compliance

24.1.12 If it is not practical to conduct a scheduled mediation session because a party fails to attend within the first 30 minutes of the time appointed for the commencement of the session, the mediator shall cancel the session and immediately file with the mediation co-ordinator a certificate of non-compliance (Form 24.1D).

NON-COMPLIANCE

24.1.13 (1) When a certificate of non-compliance is filed, the mediation co-ordinator shall refer the matter to a case management master or case management judge.

(2) The case management master or case management judge may convene a case conference under subrule 77.13(1), and may,

(a) establish a timetable for the action;
(b) strike out any document filed by a party;
(c) dismiss the action, if the non-complying party is a plaintiff, or strike out the statement of defence, if that party is a defendant;
(d) order a party to pay costs;
(e) make any other order that is just.

(3) Subrules 77.13(7) and 77.14(9) do not apply to the case conference.

CONFIDENTIALITY

24.1.14 All communications at a mediation session and the mediator's notes and records shall be deemed to be without prejudice settlement discussions.

OUTCOME OF MEDIATION

Mediator's Report

24.1.15 (1) Within 10 days after the mediation is concluded, the mediator shall give the mediation co-ordinator and the parties a report on the mediation.

(2) The mediation co-ordinator for the county may remove from the list maintained under subrule 24.1.08(1) the name of a mediator who does not comply with subrule (1).

Agreement

(3) If there is an agreement resolving some or all of the issues in dispute, it shall be signed by the parties or their lawyers.

(4) If the agreement settles the action, the defendant shall file a notice to that effect,

(a) in the case of an unconditional agreement, within 10 days after the agreement is signed;

(b) in the case of a conditional agreement, within 10 days after the condition is satisfied.

Failure to Comply with Signed Agreement

(5) Where a party to a signed agreement fails to comply with its terms, any other party to the agreement may,

(a) make a motion to a judge for judgment in the terms of the agreement, and the judge may grant judgment accordingly; or

(b) continue the action as if there had been no agreement.

CONSENT ORDER FOR ADDITIONAL MEDIATION SESSION

24.1.16 (1) With the consent of the parties the court may, at any stage in the action, make an order requiring the parties to participate in an additional mediation session.

(2) The court may include any necessary directions in the order.

(3) Rules 24.1.09 to 24.1.15 apply in respect of the additional session, with necessary modifications.

REVOCATION

24.1.17 This Rule is revoked on July 4, 2001.

FORM 24.1A
(General heading)
NOTICE OF NAME OF MEDIATOR AND DATE OF SESSION

TO: MEDIATION CO-ORDINATOR

1. I certify that I have consulted with the parties and that the parties have chosen the following mediator for the mediation session required by Rule 24.1: (*name*)

2. The mediator is named in the list of mediators for (*name county*).

(or)

2. The mediator is not named in a list of mediators, but has been chosen by the parties under clause 24.1.08(2)(a) or (c).

3. The mediation session will take place on (*date*).

(*Date*)   (*Name, address, telephone number and fax number of plaintiff's lawyer or of plaintiff*)

FORM 24.1B
(*General heading*)
NOTICE BY ASSIGNED MEDIATOR

TO:
AND TO:

The notice of name of mediator and date of session (Form 24.1A) required by rule 24.1.09 of the *Rules of Civil Procedure* has not been filed in this action. Accordingly, the mediation co-ordinator has assigned me to conduct the mediation session under Rule 24.1. I am a mediator named in the list of mediators for (*name county*).

The mediation session will take place on (*date*), from (*time*) to (*time*), at (*place*).

Unless the court orders otherwise, you are required to attend this mediation session. If you have a lawyer representing you in this action, he or she is also required to attend.

You are required to file a statement of issues (Form 24.1C) by (*date*) (7 days before the mediation session). A blank copy of the form is attached.

When you attend the mediation session, you should bring with you any documents that you consider of central importance in the action. You should plan to remain throughout the scheduled time. If you need another person's approval before agreeing to a settlement, you should make arrangements before the mediation session to ensure that you have ready telephone access to that person throughout the session, even outside regular business hours.

YOU MAY BE PENALIZED UNDER RULE 24.1.13 IF YOU FAIL TO FILE A STATEMENT OF ISSUES OR FAIL TO ATTEND THE MEDIATION SESSION.

(*Date*)   (*Name, address, telephone number and fax number of mediator*)

cc. Mediation co-ordinator

FORM 24.1C
(*General heading*)
STATEMENT OF ISSUES

(*To be provided to mediator and parties at least seven days before the mediation session*)

1. Factual and legal issues in dispute

The plaintiff (*or* defendant) states that the following factual and legal issues are in dispute and remain to be resolved.

(*Issues should be stated briefly and numbered consecutively.*)

2. Party's position and interests (what the party hopes to achieve)

(*Brief summary.*)

3. Attached documents

Attached to this form are the following documents that the plaintiff (*or* defendant) considers of central importance in the action: (*list*)

(*date*)　　　　　　　　　　　　　(*party's signature*)

　　　　　　　　　　　　　　　　(*Name, address, telephone number and fax number of lawyer of party filing statement of issues, or of party*)

NOTE: When the plaintiff provides a copy of this form to the mediator, a copy of the pleadings shall also be included.

NOTE: Rule 24.1.14 provides as follows:

All communications at a mediation session and the mediator's notes and records shall be deemed to be without prejudice settlement discussions.

FORM 24.1D
(*General heading*)
CERTIFICATE OF NON-COMPLIANCE

TO: MEDIATION CO-ORDINATOR

I, (*name*), mediator, certify that this certificate of non-compliance is filed because:

( )　(*Identify party(ies)*) failed to provide a copy of a statement of issues to the mediator and the other parties (*or* to the mediator *or* to *party(ies)*).

( )　(*Identify plaintiff*) failed to provide a copy of the pleadings to the mediator.

( )　(*Identify party(ies)*) failed to attend within the first 30 minutes of a scheduled mediation session.

(*Date*)　(*Name, address, telephone number and fax number, if any, of mediator*)

NOTE: Forms 24.1A, 24.1B, 24.1C and 24.1D are revoked on July 4, 2001.

NOTE: Part I of Tariff A to the *Rules of Civil Procedure* is amended by adding the following item (to be revoked July 1, 2001):

1.1   Preparation and attendance at mediation under Rule 24.1, for each party represented, up to..$300

An increased fee may be allowed in the discretion of the assessment officer.

NOTE: Part II of Tariff A to the *Rules of Civil Procedure* is amended by adding the following item (to be revoked July 1, 2001):

23.1 Fees actually paid to a mediator in accordance with (*identify regulation*) made under the *Administration of Justice Act.*

APPENDIX 4.5
O. REG. 451/98
MEDIATORS' FEES (RULE 24.1, RULES OF CIVIL PROCEDURE)

As amended to O. Reg. 447/00

1. In this Regulation,

"mandatory mediation session" means the mediation session required by Rule 24.1 of the Rules of Civil Procedure.

2. For the purposes of this Regulation,

(a) two or more plaintiffs shall be deemed to be one party; and

(b) two or more defendants who jointly serve a statement of defence or are jointly represented shall be deemed to be one party.

3. (1) When a mandatory mediation session is conducted under Rule 24.1 of the Rules of Civil Procedure by a mediator named in a list described in subrule 24.1.08(1) of those Rules, fees shall be paid in accordance with this Regulation.

(2) The mediator's fees for the mandatory mediation session cover the following services:

1.   One-half hour of preparation time for each party.

2.   Up to three hours of actual mediation.

4. (1) The mediator's fees for the mandatory mediation session shall not exceed the amount shown in the following Table.

TABLE

Number of Parties	Maximum Fees
2	$600 plus GST
3	$675 plus GST
4	$750 plus GST
5 or more	$825 plus GST

(2) Each party is required to pay an equal share of the mediator's fees for the mandatory mediation session.

(3) After the first three hours of actual mediation, the mediation may be continued if the parties and the mediator agree to do so and agree on the mediator's fees or hourly rate for the additional time.

5. (1) If the mediator cancels a session under subrule 24.1.10(5) of the Rules of Civil Procedure because a party fails to comply with subrule 24.1.10(1), that party shall pay any cancellation fees.

(2) If the mediator cancels a session under subrule 24.1.12(1) of the Rules of Civil Procedure because a party fails to attend within the first 30 minutes of the session, the party who fails to attend shall pay any cancellation fees.

(3) Two or more parties who fail to comply or to attend, as the case may be, shall pay the cancellation fees in equal shares.

(4) The cancellation fees shall not exceed the applicable amount shown in the Table to subsection 4(1).

6. A party's failure to pay a share referred to in subsection 4(2) or 5(3) does not increase the share or shares of the other party or parties.

7. (1) A party who holds a valid legal aid certificate with respect to the proceeding is not required to pay fees under this Regulation.

(2) A party to whom subsection (1) does not apply but who may suffer financial hardship if required to pay fees under this Regulation may contact the mediation co-ordinator.

8. Sections 1 to 7 are revoked on July 4, 2001.

9. This Regulation comes into force on January 4, 1999.

Arbitration

Key Concepts

- Arbitration uses a neutral adjudicator (trier of fact), a presentation of evidence, and a binding adjudication of the dispute by the adjudicator.
- Arbitration may be mandated by an administrative tribunal such as the Financial Services Commission of Ontario and other insurance commissions in Canada.
- Arbitration can also be used where the disputing parties have voluntarily agreed to accept a third party arbitrator's decision as an alternative to litigation. Voluntary arbitration is now becoming widespread in the insurance industry.
- Arbitration is governed by procedural rules.
- Evidence may be presented orally or through documentation. Oral evidence may be given by first-hand witnesses or by expert witnesses. Every witness should be prepared prior to testifying, and should act professionally and answer all questions honestly.
- Documentary evidence is an integral part of the arbitration process and is subject to particular rules of evidence.
- Arbitrations may be subject to judicial review if the arbitrator exceeds his or her jurisdiction or makes an error in law.
- Arbitration does not necessarily include discovery. Pre-hearing disclosure of documents is typically agreed to by the parties or does not occur.
- Arbitration fees are charged by the day, and there is a charge for adjournments and cancellations. Legal costs are not generally awarded for arbitrations, so

the successful party does not necessarily recoup expenses incurred to protect its position.

- Because arbitration is private, it does not necessarily have the precedential value of a court award.

1. AN ARBITRATION PRIMER

The other forms of alternative dispute resolution which have been discussed in this book are consensus-based, particularly negotiation and mediation. Arbitration is an adversarial process involving the presentation of evidence to a neutral third party who imposes a decision or award on the disputants.

Arbitration may be mandated by statute, or the disputants may voluntarily agree to it. Many dispute resolution clauses appearing in insurance policies and other contractual arrangements contain a staged dispute resolution mechanism including mediation and arbitration (see Chapter 6 for more discussion regarding dispute resolution clauses).

(a) Characteristics of Arbitration

Voluntary/mandated: There are situations where arbitration is mandated by statute or by regulation. However, the parties may also voluntarily decide to use arbitration as a direct alternative to traditional litigation in the civil courts.

Binding: Litigation may result in a court award which is directly enforceable through the courts. Some arbitration statutes may also provide mechanisms for the enforcement of arbitration decisions in the courts, or the parties may agree contractually to be bound by the arbitrator's decision. Some parties have included as part of their agreement to arbitrate the ability to enforce the award in the courts.

Accessibility: Where the parties have voluntarily agreed to arbitrate, they may grant powers to the arbitrator which are more comprehensive or flexible than the remedial powers of the courts.

(b) Choice of Arbitrator

One of the primary differences between private and public litigation is the ability to choose the third party intervenor or arbitrator. Parties to a dispute may prefer arbitration so they can choose a well-respected arbitrator with special expertise in the disputed subject area as opposed to being assigned a judge whose identity will not be known until the time of trial.

(c) Arbitration Logistics

Arbitrations are generally conducted in a meeting room, not dissimilar to a mediation. Long tables are set up to accommodate the parties, with the arbitrator or arbitration panel sitting at the head of the room. Hearings are sometimes conducted in hotels, so some attention should be paid to informing hotel staff as to how to set up the tables. A hollow square is preferable to a T-formation because it allows for plenty of room to spread out exhibits, notebooks and briefs.

Very often, the arbitrator will require a notice of hearing. A record of who will be appearing can be prepared ahead of time and should include:

(a) the style of cause;
(b) a heading indicating appearances on behalf of the party;
(c) the name and address of counsel; and
(d) at the parties' discretion, the name of the client or representative who will be attending.

Copies should be made available to the arbitrator or panel and to opposing counsel.

Arbitrations can be quite informal. It is not unusual to have coffee and/or refreshments available throughout the arbitration.

Arbitrators charge daily fees, as well as fees for adjournments and cancellations. Legal costs are not generally awarded for arbitrations, so the successful party does not necessarily recoup expenses incurred to protect its position. Also, because arbitration is private, it does not necessarily have the precedential value of a court award.

2. GENERIC STEPS OF AN ARBITRATION

(a) Pre-Arbitration Process

Typically, a legal issue arises where the parties take opposing or adverse positions over a defined and articulated dispute, and adjudication by a neutral third party is sought. The parties may choose to go through the traditional litigation system in the courts. On the other hand, they may be mandated by law or by a policy/contract provision, or they may voluntarily choose to pursue arbitration. The pre-hearing stages of an arbitration generally include:

(a) choice of forum and proceeding;
(b) formal commencement of the originating process;
(c) response;
(d) intervening resolution attempts; and
(e) pre-hearing disclosure.

These stages may take months or years depending on the forum or the particulars of the dispute.

Choice of forum and proceeding: The decision to use arbitration is dependent on many factors. Arbitration may be included in a policy as the contractual choice of forum to resolve disputes; it may be mandated as a sequential step following mediation (this is illustrated by the processes at various insurance commissions across Canada); or the parties may mutually agree to use private arbitration as opposed to traditional litigation. The criteria used to determine the choice of process are more fully discussed at pp. 11-14.

Originating process: The originating process for arbitration may be an application to a tribunal, as in the case of the Financial Services Commission of Ontario, or an exchange of letters indicating the intention of the parties to go to private arbitration. Generally, the originating process identifies the parties, the nature of the dispute, the issues, and the remedy sought. The originating process is delivered to each opposing party according to the rules of the process, and a response from each is required.

Response: The arbitration process generally requires a response from each party opposing the claimant or complainant in the dispute. The response in the insurance context is generally formal and in writing, similar to a statement of defence in civil proceedings. Once every response is received, the dispute, subject to intervening resolution attempts and some element of disclosure between the parties of evidence or of particulars, can be advanced to arbitration.

Intervening resolution attempts: At any stage in the life of a legal dispute, the dispute may be withdrawn by the complainant or claimant, or it may be resolved by agreement between or among the parties. Negotiation and mediation attempts as discussed in Chapters 3 and 4 may be used.

Pre-hearing disclosure of evidence: Most arbitration processes include some mechanism for at least partial disclosure of evidence to the opposing party or parties. In the case of mandated arbitration, this may be prescribed by the governing or enabling legislation. Pre-hearing meetings may be conducted by the arbitrator or by another neutral to canvass settlement discussions with the parties. The arbitrators at the Financial Services Commission of Ontario are trained to mediate disputes, and typically the parties first meet with an arbitrator who will not ultimately be assigned to the full and formal hearing. In a private arbitration, this step is subject to the consent and agreed processes of the parties. If the parties choose to use the arbitrator as a mediator, this is sometimes referred to as Med-Arb or Mediation-Arbitration. This should be carefully considered by the parties and consented to in advance. There is some controversy in the dispute resolution community as to whether a mediator should also arbitrate the case. However, this is subject to agreement between the parties.

(b) Basic Principles of Arbitration

Most arbitrations in Canada are adversarial in nature. The parties who are adverse to each other present to a neutral third party, trier of fact or arbitrator evidence and legal argument supporting their position. Once all the relevant and admissible evidence has been presented and the legal position and supporting arguments of each party have been heard, the arbitrator makes a decision and imposes the result on all the parties to the dispute.

The neutral third party who hears and determines the arbitration, the arbitrator, may be a single person or a panel. The arbitrator may be assigned in certain mandated arbitrations. Where there is choice, the choice of arbitrator is determined by the nature of the dispute, the type of law at issue, and the forum. The powers of the arbitrator are status-, context- and forum-specific. In other words, arbitrators may have different qualifications and may be appointed differently than a judge. Further, they have different jurisdictions with different powers. Some arbitrators derive their powers and jurisdiction by statute. In all cases, subject to the statutory or customary rules of the forum, the arbitrator is in charge of the conduct and procedure of the hearing. He or she enforces the rules, sets the tone, swears in the witnesses, and determines any issue in dispute. At the end of the proceeding, the arbitrator is empowered to impose a decision based on the evidence, the applicable law, and legal principles. Often this decision is written and incorporates the arbitrator's reasons.

Two requirements in an arbitration will generally determine the outcome. In most arbitrations, one party bears the burden of proof or the legal responsibility to prove, on the applicable legal standard of proof, the elements of the claim in dispute. The initial and major burden is generally borne by one side, but the burden may shift to the other side in certain circumstances. As a general rule, the party with the initial burden of proof is the side alleging the breach. Once that burden is discharged on the applicable legal standard, the other side may have a corresponding burden to prove some other element such as a defence, a mitigating circumstance, or a legally sufficient excuse for the conduct in issue. The legal standard is the law's measurement of the extent of the burden of proof a party must discharge or meet in order to prove its case. Typically, the legal standard in an arbitration is "on a balance of probabilities".

(c) Conduct of the Hearing

The general format for most arbitrations is as follows:

(a) opening statement;
(b) presentation of evidence, including documentary evidence and the examination and cross-examination of direct and expert witnesses;
(c) summation and legal argument; and
(d) decision by the adjudicator. Following release of a decision, the parties may apply it as rendered, or the decision may be appealed by one or all of the parties.

Opening statement: Most arbitrations commence with each party to the dispute, through legal representatives, making an opening statement to the arbitrator. This statement is a summary of the anticipated evidence which each side will present and each side's legal view of the case. Every party has an opportunity to make an opening statement, which provides the arbitrator with a framework of the issues at stake. The next step is for each party to present evidence supporting its legal position or view.

Evidence: With a few exceptions, the party bearing the onus of proof generally presents all of its evidence first. This is followed by a presentation of all the evidence from the opposing party or parties. The original party then has a limited right to respond or reply with further evidence which speaks to any new issues raised or evidence presented by the opposition. Evidence is generally oral or documentary, and it may be direct, circumstantial or expert. Types of evidence and the presentation of evidence are discussed more fully at p. 117. Particular statutory rules apply in each forum to determine what evidence is admissible, on what basis, and for what purpose, and may also determine what evidence is not admissible. Once the presentation of evidence is complete, each party sums up its case in a closing statement.

Summation and legal argument: This is an opportunity for the parties and their representatives to review their positions against the evidence and everyone's theory of the case. Each party reviews and argues before the arbitrator the applicable law and legal precedents which best support its legal position and theory of the case. Once again, the party presenting first has a limited right of reply or response to any new arguments or precedents raised by the opposition.

Decision: The decision of the arbitrator can take many forms. Arbitrators generally issue awards and written decisions with reasons that may or may not be published. Typically, arbitration awards in the insurance context are private unless otherwise agreed by the parties. Most arbitrators have a defined jurisdiction to impose certain remedies or sanctions. The arbitrator's award is usually legally binding on the parties upon release, and it is enforceable in law. However, the decision cannot exceed the jurisdiction of the arbitrator, nor can it be based on errors of law. Otherwise, it may be subject to judicial review or appeal.

Judicial review: If the decision of an arbitrator or tribunal is based on an error in law or exceeds the jurisdiction of the arbitrator, it may be taken to judicial review with a view to having it overturned or quashed. In very limited circumstances, errors in fact may be appealable, although generally judicial review requires an error in law or jurisdiction. A judicial review is usually conducted through written briefs and legal argument, and rarely includes oral evidence.

(d) Procedural Matters

(i) *Orders*

Arbitration is very similar to litigation in that orders may be made:

(a) requiring notice of the parties;
(b) excluding witnesses;
(c) requiring particulars; or
(d) permitting/disallowing adjournments.

In order for the arbitrator to make such orders, the document referring the parties to arbitration must confirm the power of the arbitrator to govern the procedure of the hearing. This often includes the ability to make binding rulings in respect of that procedure.[1]

---

[1] Please note that there are federal and provincial statutes governing arbitration. A complete list is included in Appendix 5.1 at the end of this chapter.

Since arbitrations are less formal than court proceedings, it is not industry practice to produce motion materials. If a preliminary procedural issue must be raised, this is generally done orally. Very often, these kinds of issues are dealt with through a telephone conference prior to the arbitration itself. The parties may also choose to make submissions and file authorities.

(ii) *Evidence*

The evidence at an arbitration will include witnesses with first-hand testimony, experts, and documentary evidence. Documentary evidence may include records, letters, memos, tapes, videos, charts, photographs and any other tangible record of the event that may be legally admissible.

To be admissible, evidence must generally be relevant to the issues or events, must be admissible based on common law standards and considerations, and must meet the statutory rules of evidence and the jurisdiction. The parties may agree in advance to the admission of particular evidence. This would be part of the originating process or referral to arbitration.

One of the biggest differences between litigation and arbitration is the speed at which the evidence is presented. Typically, the arbitrator will transcribe testimony in long-hand or on a laptop computer. It is uncommon, unless arrangements are made and fees negotiated in advance, to have a court reporter. Because of this, it is critical that counsel and witnesses speak slowly and monitor whether the arbitrator's note-taking is parallel with what the speaker is saying. Otherwise, evidence may be lost. All witnesses should be advised of this beforehand so they can address the arbitrator in a suitable manner. This also applies to the speed with which advocates present their opening remarks and argument.

While the rules of evidence which will be applied should be addressed in the referral to arbitration, generally arbitrators take a liberal view of what evidence is admissible, and they may admit hearsay or material of arguable relevance. They may listen to objections, but in general, they admit the testimony with the proviso that it may receive little weight in the final analysis. One practitioner recommends that despite the arbitrator's inaction on objections, it is probably wise to object in any event and to keep the submissions on admissibility brief in order to avoid passive acceptance or non-objection being perceived as a waiver.[2]

Advocates should remember that the informality inherent in an arbitration can be misleading. Issues such as fairness to witnesses and prejudice to one party or another will be taken seriously. Expert witnesses must still be qualified, and opinion evidence may be restricted.

With regard to documentary evidence, sufficient copies should be made for the arbitrator/panel, opposing counsel and the witness. While copies can generally be made at the arbitration proper, this can slow up the process if the parties have to wait while the copies are made.

---

[2] Maureen Farson, "Participating in an Arbitration" (presented at the 1997 Institute of Continuing Legal Education, Canadian Bar Association – Ontario, Toronto, February 1, 1997).

(iii) *The Arbitration Agreement*

Once the parties have decided to proceed by way of arbitration rather than litigation, it is necessary to prepare a written arbitration agreement. This is applicable whether the arbitration procedure was agreed upon at the beginning of the dispute, or whether the parties commenced traditional litigation and decided at some stage in that process to switch to arbitration.

The purpose behind an arbitration agreement is to set forth the ground rules under which the arbitration will be held. It is important to understand that the arbitration process is an extremely flexible one and, to a very large degree, can be whatever the parties want it to be. The statutory framework for arbitration agreements in Ontario is the *Arbitration Act, 1991*.[3] This Act sets out a number of "default" provisions with respect to the terms and procedures of an arbitration. However, the parties can contract out of almost all these provisions and create their own.

Since most of the lawyers who practise in the field of insurance are civil litigators, many are more comfortable with an arbitration agreement modelled after the process they know best, that is, the litigation process as set out in the *Rules of Civil Procedure*.[4] The "Model Arbitration Agreement" in Appendix 5.3 uses the *Rules of Civil Procedure* as a framework, but it allows the parties to pick and choose which parts of the Rules apply and to create new procedures where the situation warrants. It allows the parties to choose among various options on selected clauses. For instance, the parties could choose to have discoveries just like in a lawsuit, to dispense completely with discoveries, or to have limited discoveries. The choices provided in the model agreement are only intended to give some ideas. They are not intended to be exhaustive, but are designed to provide examples of areas that should be considered. Examples of clauses where options can be negotiated are set out in Appendix 5.2.

Negotiating an arbitration agreement should not be a lengthy or complicated procedure. A short meeting of the lawyers can usually result in an agreement. The signatures of the clients are not necessary since the lawyers can sign on behalf of their clients. A copy of the signed agreement should be forwarded to the arbitrator prior to the hearing.

(iv) *Conduct of the Witnesses*

Given that the conduct of an arbitration and the presentation of evidence are very similar to what happens in a civil proceeding, this chapter will not give a lot of detail about examining and cross-examining witnesses, or strategizing about the provision of documents. Suffice to say that attention should be paid to the agreement to arbitrate as it will impact strategy.

---

[3] S.O. 1991, c. 17.
[4] R.R.O. 1990, Reg. 194.

As in any adversarial process, witnesses should be prepared. They should be advised not to discuss the case with others and to review all relevant documentation prior to testifying. It is usually mandated that witnesses meet with the representative who requested their attendance in order to prepare and review the evidence. Witnesses should be informed as to what the expectations of attendance are in terms of date, time, place and particulars, as well as the length of attendance if this can be determined. There should be a verification as to what fees or reimbursement of expenses will apply. Witnesses should be made aware of the need to take an oath or to affirm that it is their intention to tell the truth, and of the fact that they will be subject to examination, cross-examination and redirect as in the civil system.

Some suggestions for witnesses appearing before arbitrators include the following:

(1)   Dress and act professionally.

(2)   Make eye contact with the person asking questions. Staring at the floor or ceiling rarely invokes the arbitrator's confidence.

(3)   Speak slowly, clearly and loudly. A whispered 20-minute ramble will not be remembered, let alone credited.

(4)   Use simple language and explain any technical terms or phrases that the arbitrator may not understand.

(5)   Ask for clarification if a question is not understood. Answering the wrong question may leave a poor impression with the arbitrator.

(6)   Do not be belligerent or aggressive with the questioner. Despite the informality of arbitration, aggressive conduct can break the decorum of the proceedings and is rarely considered professional or appropriate.

(7)   Do not take a demeaning attitude. Some legal representatives may take that attitude. However, witnesses are rarely accorded that luxury.

(8)   Explain everything. Do not assume that the arbitrator knows all the facts. Hopefully, the legal representative will assist by requesting an explanation if necessary.

(9)   Be forthright and honest. This reflects a professional and credible witness.

(10) Speak from personal knowledge. Speculation is for the adjudicator or the expert, not for the ordinary witness.

(11) Do not guess at an answer. If the correct answer is "I don't know", that should be the answer given.

(12) If the answer is unlikely to assist the party the witness is supporting, the answer should be given honestly anyway. Damage control is properly the purview of the legal representative, and the answer might simply require some clarification. Let the lawyer decide.

(13) Avoid conjecture and innuendo. They are not the basis of personal knowledge and observation.

(v) *Expert Witnesses*

As in a civil proceeding, expert testimony may be accepted in an arbitration. The expert is hired by one or more of the parties to the proceeding and hence is not neutral. He or she is chosen on the basis of knowledge, expertise and credentials.

After being provided with information about the circumstances, the expert is asked to render a written opinion, in the form of a report, on a particular issue or issues. The report may be an opinion about specific issues, or it may be a response to the opposing party's expert report or opinion. If the expert is to be used in a legal proceeding, the report must be submitted to opposing counsel in advance of the hearing. This gives opposing counsel the opportunity to examine it and to arrange counter-evidence.

Procedural rules require that an expert witness be qualified in a particular area. It is up to the legal representative who retained the witness to establish for the arbitrator or arbitration panel that witness's qualifications. Opposing counsel can question or discredit such qualifications and expertise or can accept them. Ultimately, the arbitrator accepts or rejects the expert witness. If rejected, the witness cannot testify. If the arbitrator resists on the matter, the witness may be allowed to testify, but the arbitrator may later discount or ignore the witness's opinion.

Expert witnesses are paid for their time and expertise. The responsibility for remuneration rests with the person calling the witness.

APPENDIX 5.1
ARBITRATION LEGISLATION IN CANADA

Federal

Commercial Arbitration Act, R.S.C. 1985, c. 17 (2nd Supp.)

Alberta

Arbitration Act, S.A. 1991, c. A-43.1

British Columbia

Commercial Arbitration Act, R.S.B.C. 1996, c. 55

Manitoba

Arbitration Act, S.M. 1997, c. 4 (C.C.S.M., c. A120)

New Brunswick

Arbitration Act, S.N.B. 1992, c. A-10.1

Newfoundland

Arbitration Act, R.S.N. 1990, c. A-14

Northwest Territories

Arbitration Act, R.S.N.W.T. 1988, c. A-5

Nova Scotia

Arbitration Act, R.S.N.S. 1989, c. 19

Commercial Arbitration Act, S.N.S. 1999, c. 5

Ontario

Arbitration Act, 1991, S.O. 1991, c. 17

Prince Edward Island

Arbitration Act, R.S.P.E.I. 1988, c. A-16 (repealed and replaced by 1996, c. 4 – not proclaimed)

Quebec

No legislation

Saskatchewan

Arbitration Act, 1992, S.S. 1992, c. A-24.1

Yukon

Arbitration Act, R.S.Y. 1986, c. 7

APPENDIX 5.2
ARBITRATION AGREEMENT CLAUSES
WITH SUGGESTIONS FOR ALTERNATIVE CLAUSES

APPLICABILITY OF THE ARBITRATION ACT, 1991[5]

The provisions of the Arbitration Act, 1991, S.O. 1991, c. 17 apply to this arbitration except where a provision of the Agreement applies otherwise.

This is a standard provision setting out the statutory framework .

MISCELLANEOUS PROVISIONS

Wherever the Rules refer to a "Judge", "Master", "Registrar" or "Court", they shall be read as if they read "the Arbitrator".

---

[5] Enforcement of arbitration awards by the courts is statute-driven. For example, if the parties agree, as in this sample clause, to be bound by the Ontario *Arbitration Act, 1991*, then s. 50(8) of that Act allows the courts the same powers to enforce an arbitrator's award as to enforce one of the court's own judgments. Disputants who wish to enforce the award serve to the court an application of enforcement with an attachment of the original award or a certified copy.

Wherever the Rules refer to "the Plaintiff", they shall be read as if they read "the Insured".

Wherever the Rules refer to "the Defendant", they shall be read as if they read "the Insurer".

This Agreement may not be amended except by written document signed by either the parties or their counsel.

DEFINITIONS

"Act" means the Arbitration Act, 1991, S.O. 1991, c. 17.

"Rules" means the Rules of Civil Procedure, R.R.O. 1990, Reg. 194.

These provisions incorporate the Rules of Civil Procedure into the Arbitration Agreement.

ISSUES IN DISPUTE

The Plaintiff and the Defendant agree to submit the following matters to binding arbitration on the terms set out in this Agreement:

- *liability;*
- *the determination of all moneys owing to the Plaintiff;*
- *a determination as to whether or not the Policy dated September 1, 1992 is enforceable.*

– or –

The Plaintiff and Defendant agree to submit to binding arbitration all matters arising from the cessation of the Insured's coverage with the Insurer on the terms set out in this Agreement.

If the parties desire, they can limit the arbitration to certain disputes only, in which case the first clause would be appropriate. If there is no such limitation, then the second clause can be used.

ACCEPTED FACTS AND LAW

The following will be taken as proven facts and/or law in the Arbitration:

- *The Plaintiff reasonably mitigated his damages.*
- *The Arbitrator is not to apply the doctrines of either near cause or ball park justice.*

This clause allows the parties to either agree that certain facts will not need to be proven or to define what the law on a certain subject is agreed to be. It can also be used to limit the powers of the arbitrator, *e.g.*, by agreeing that the arbitrator cannot award punitive damages.

SELECTING AN ARBITRATOR

The Arbitrator shall be   . However, if she is unable to accept the appointment, the parties agree to   as the Arbitrator.

– or –

The parties shall endeavour to agree upon an Arbitrator within 30 days of the date upon which this Agreement is signed. If no such Agreement is forthcoming, either party may apply under s. 10 of the Arbitration Act, 1991 for the Court to select an Arbitrator.

Perhaps one of the biggest advantages to arbitration is that the parties get to choose their own adjudicator. Anyone the parties agree upon can arbitrate. Thus the parties could choose a lawyer who practises in the area, an established arbitrator, a retired judge, or anyone else. The names and biographies of established arbitrators are available through sources such as:

(a)   Alternative Dispute Resolution Directory
       Published by:

> ADR Section of the Canadian Bar Association – Ontario
> 20 Toronto St., Toronto, Ontario
> Tel.: (416) 869-1047

This directory is also available at:

> Alternate Dispute Resolution Centre of the Ontario Superior Court of Justice
> 77 Grenville St., Suite 800, Toronto, Ontario

(b)   Arbitration & Mediation Institute of Ontario Inc.
       234 Eglinton Ave. East, Suite 303, Toronto, Ontario
       Tel.: (416) 487-4447

If for some reason the parties cannot agree on an arbitrator, the second clause allows the parties to apply to a court and to choose the arbitrator. Ideally the parties in a voluntary private arbitration should choose the arbitrator.

TIME AND LOCATION OF ARBITRATION HEARING

The Arbitration hearing shall take place in the City of Toronto, at a location to be selected by the Arbitrator.

The Arbitration shall be held on the following dates:

– or –

The Arbitrator shall set the dates for the hearing after consultation with the parties.

Agreeing on the city where the arbitration will take place can be very important if the parties reside in different cities. Similarly, the timing can be very important to one or both of the parties. If the parties cannot agree on the dates, it is suggested that this be left up to the arbitrator, as set out in the third clause.

PLEADINGS

The parties agree to not have pleadings of any sort.

– or –

The parties agree to not have pleadings as described in the Rules, but do agree to exchange written statements which indicate their positions, the points at issue, and the relief sought. These statements are to be exchanged by September 25, 1992.

– or –

The parties agree to exchange pleadings in accordance with Rules 25, 26, 27 and 28. The pleadings shall be filed with the Arbitrator rather than the Court.

– or –

The parties agree to exchange pleadings in accordance with Rules 25, 26, 27 and 28, subject to the following provision:
*   *The period for service for all pleadings shall be 10 days.*

– or –

The parties agree that the pleadings already exchanged shall be used in the Arbitration.

This clause gives options to choose from with respect to pleadings. Only one of these would be included in any arbitration agreement.

DOCUMENTS

The parties agree that Rule 30 shall apply.

– or –

The parties agree to exchange copies of all documents they wish to rely upon at the Arbitration no later than 30 days prior to the Arbitration hearing. Documents not produced within that time frame may only be used at the Arbitration hearing with leave of the Arbitrator.

– or –

The parties agree that neither party will exchange documents or be obligated to advise the other party as to what documents it intends to rely upon at the Arbitration hearing.

– or –

The parties agree that Rule 30 shall apply subject to the following provision:
*   *Unless one party specifically requests the other party to produce the original of a document, each party may use photocopies.*

This clause provides options regarding disclosure, ranging from an obligation to prepare an Affidavit of Documents as set forth in Rule 30 of the *Rules of Civil*

Procedure, to having no document disclosure requirements at all. Only one of these options would be included in any arbitration agreement.

MOTIONS AND INTERIM MATTERS

The parties agree that Rules 37 and 39 apply except that all Motions shall be heard at a location selected by the Arbitrator.

– or –

The parties agree that the Arbitrator shall rule on all procedural matters arising before the first hearing date. The Arbitrator shall set the procedure for the resolution of these matters.

– or –

The parties agree that the Arbitrator shall rule on all procedural matters arising before the first hearing date. All such matters shall be submitted to the Arbitrator in writing. The Arbitrator shall provide a brief written award within 10 days of receipt of the parties' submissions. No hearing on these matters shall be permitted unless specifically requested by the Arbitrator.

This clause provides for three different approaches to having the arbitrator resolve interim or interlocutory disputes. Only one of these options would be included in any arbitration agreement.

EXAMINATIONS FOR DISCOVERY

The parties agree to not have examinations for discovery.

– or –

The parties agree to have examinations for discovery in accordance with Rules 31, 32, 33, 34, 35 and 36.

– or –

The parties agree to have examinations for discovery in accordance with Rules 31, 32, 33, 34, 35 and 36, subject to the following provisions:
- *The discoveries shall be held in Toronto on October 15 and 16, 1992.*
- *Each party is to be entitled to a maximum of 5 hours to conduct its discovery.*

– or –

The parties agree that the examinations for discovery already held can be used in the Arbitration.

There are four options to choose from, depending on how important the parties feel the discoveries are. The last clause is only applicable where discoveries have already been held as part of a traditional lawsuit and the parties decide, in the course of the lawsuit, that they want to switch to arbitration.

EVIDENCE AT THE ARBITRATION HEARING

The Arbitrator shall apply the laws of evidence as if the hearing was a trial in the Ontario Superior Court of Justice, including the provisions of Rule 53.

– or –

The Arbitrator shall apply the laws of evidence as if the hearing was a labour arbitration under the Labour Relations Act, 1995, S.O. 1995, c. 1, Sch. A.

– or –

The Arbitrator shall apply the laws of evidence as if the hearing was a trial in the Ontario Superior Court of Justice, subject to the following provisions:

- *The hearsay rule shall be applied as if the hearing was a labour arbitration under the Labour Relations Act, 1995.*
- *The parties may rely on photocopies of originals.*
- *No notice under the Evidence Act, R.S.O. 1990, c. E.23, is required for business records.*
- *All expert reports shall be served on the other party at least 30 days prior to the date of the hearing.*

– or –

The parties shall not be permitted to present oral evidence. Rather, they are restricted to presenting the following evidence:

- *documents;*
- *expert reports;*
- *transcripts of examinations;*
- *witness statements.*

The parties are entitled to utilize the provisions of Rule 51 (Admissions).

There is a general misconception among many lawyers that the laws of evidence either do not apply to arbitrations or are interpreted in a much looser manner than they would be in a courtroom before a trial judge. This is inaccurate, as the parties can tell the arbitrator whether he or she is to act like a trial judge with respect to the admission of evidence or whether some other standard is to apply. This clause provides a number of options to choose from. Again, only one clause should be chosen for any particular arbitration agreement, except with respect to the last clause on the use of Rule 51. This clause can be combined with any of the other clauses.

REMEDIAL POWERS OF THE ARBITRATOR

The Arbitrator shall have all the remedial powers of a trial judge of the Ontario Superior Court of Justice.

– or –

The Arbitrator shall be limited in her remedial powers to:
- *awarding monetary damages for lost income and benefits during the appropriate notice period;*
- *awarding damages for mental distress to a maximum of $5,000;*
- *awarding punitive damages to a maximum of $10,000;*
- *awarding prejudgment interest.*

This clause allows the parties to restrict or expand the remedial powers of the arbitrator. This is a hallmark of the arbitration process.

OFFERS TO SETTLE

Rule 49 applies to these proceedings.

– or –

Rule 49 applies to these proceedings, subject to the following provision:
- *For an offer to be operative, it must be served on the other party within 20 days of the first hearing date.*

If the parties give the arbitrator the power to award costs, they should consider whether they should use Rule 49 offers. If the parties do not want the arbitrator to award costs, then this section should be deleted.

REASONS OF THE ARBITRATOR

The Arbitrator is to give written reasons in her award.

– or –

The Arbitrator is not to give written reasons in her award.

The parties may not want written reasons for a number of reasons, including cost, timelines of the decision, and avoidance of a written record of embarrassing evidence or adverse findings of credibility. If the parties want reasons but not an opus on the law of insurance, they can agree that the arbitrator give "short" written reasons.

AWARD OF COSTS

The Arbitrator shall have no power to award costs.

– or –

The Arbitrator shall have all the power of a judge of the Ontario Superior Court of Justice to award costs, including determination of the quantum.

– or –

The Arbitrator shall have all the power of a judge of the Ontario Superior Court of Justice to award costs, including determination of the quantum, subject to the following provisions:

- *The Arbitrator may order one party to reimburse the other party, either in whole or in part, for its share of the Arbitrator's fees and disbursements.*
- *The maximum counsel fee at hearing shall be $1,500 per full day of hearing.*

Here the parties can agree to expand or limit the power of the arbitrator to award costs. This clause should be read in conjunction with the following provision, "Fees of the Arbitrator".

FEES OF THE ARBITRATOR

The parties agree to share equally the fees and disbursements of the Arbitrator, and they agree that this responsibility shall not be the subject of any order for legal costs that the Arbitrator may award.

– or –

The parties acknowledge that each of them is directly liable to the Arbitrator to pay one-half of her fees and disbursements. However, the Arbitrator may, in her award of costs, order one party to reimburse the other party for part or all of that party's share of the fees and disbursements of the Arbitrator.

One, but not both, of these clauses should be chosen. The second clause is designed to insure that the arbitrator will not be influenced by the issue of whether or not his or her arbitration account will be paid.

TRANSCRIPTS OF THE HEARING

The evidence at the arbitration hearing is to be transcribed.

– or –

The evidence at the arbitration hearing is not to be transcribed.

Unless the parties are planning to allow an appeal of the arbitrator's decision (see the following clause), it does not make sense to have the evidence transcribed. Remember that the parties will pay the full cost of the court reporter, unlike the situation at trial where the province picks up the cost of the reporter but the parties pay for the transcript.

RIGHTS OF APPEAL

The parties agree that the decision of the Arbitrator is final and binding upon the parties, and no appeal to a Court is allowed.

– or –

The parties agree that an appeal from the Arbitrator's award is allowed only on a question of law.

– or –

The parties agree that an appeal from the Arbitrator's award is allowed only on a question of law or of mixed law and fact.

– or –

The parties agree that an appeal from the Arbitrator's award is allowed on a question of fact and/or law.

Only one of these clauses should be used in a particular agreement. A big advantage of arbitration is that the parties can contract out of the right to appeal, something which cannot be done in a traditional legal action. However, even if the parties decide there is no right of appeal, the *Arbitration Act, 1991* provides that the parties cannot contract out the right of a party to bring an application for judicial review. The grounds for judicial review are quite limited, however, being generally restricted to issues such as natural justice, exceeding jurisdiction, and rendering a decision which is patently unreasonable.

EXISTING LITIGATION

The parties agree to staying the present proceeding in the Ontario Superior Court of Justice until the Arbitration award is issued. At that time, the Arbitration award shall become a consent judgment in the Court action.

– or –

The parties agree to discontinue the present proceedings in the Ontario Superior Court of Justice pursuant to Rule 23.01(c).

This clause is only applicable where there is an existing lawsuit and the parties wish to switch to arbitration. It provides for a choice of what to do with the existing lawsuit. If the second clause is chosen, the parties would have to use the procedures of the *Arbitration Act, 1991* to convert the arbitration award into an enforceable court judgment.

CONFIDENTIALITY

The parties agree to keep the outcome of these arbitration proceedings strictly confidential, except as it may be necessary to implement or enforce the Arbitrator's award.

The parties agree that the Arbitration proceedings shall not be open to the public or the media.

Arbitrations can be completely private, closed to the public and the media. This can be especially important to one or both of the parties where confidential or embarrassing information will be led in evidence. Both these clauses can be used in the same agreement since they deal with different aspects of the issue.

APPENDIX 5.3
MODEL ARBITRATION AGREEMENT
FOR INSURANCE ACTIONS IN ONTARIO[6]
INCLUDING OPTIONS FOR CLAUSES WHICH CAN BE NEGOTIATED

B E T W E E N:

Jane Doe

(the "Insured")

– and –

ABC Insurance Company

(the "Insurer")

APPLICABILITY OF THE ARBITRATION ACT, 1991

The provisions of *Arbitration Act, 1991*, S.O. 1991, c. 17 apply to this arbitration except where a provision of the Agreement applies otherwise.

MISCELLANEOUS PROVISIONS

Wherever the Rules refer to a "Judge", "Master", "Registrar" or "Court", they shall be read as if they read "the Arbitrator".

Wherever the Rules refer to "the Plaintiff", they shall be read as if they read "the Employee".

Wherever the Rules refer to "the Defendant", they shall be read as if they read "the Employer".

This Agreement may not be amended except by written document signed by either the parties or their counsel.

DEFINITIONS

"Act" means the *Arbitration Act, 1991*, S.O. 1991, c. 17.

"Rules" means the *Rules of Civil Procedure*, R.R.O. 1990, Reg. 194.

---

[6] This model arbitration agreement is adapted from an agreement produced by Barry B. Fisher, Barrister, Mediator & Arbitrator, for use in the province of Ontario. It is used with permission. For a discussion of the arbitration agreement, see p. 118.

ISSUES IN DISPUTE

The Employer and the Employee agree to submit the following matters to binding arbitration on the terms set out in this Agreement:

- the appropriate notice period to which the Employee was entitled;
- the determination of all moneys owing to the Plaintiff;
- a determination as to whether or not the Non-Competition Agreement dated September 1, 1992 is enforceable.

– or –

The Employer and the Employee agree to submit to binding arbitration all matters arising from the cessation of the Employee's employment with the Employer on the terms set out in this Agreement.

ACCEPTED FACTS AND LAW

The following will be taken as proven facts and/or law in the Arbitration.

- The Employee reasonably mitigated his damages.
- If the Employee is found by the Arbitrator to have stolen property of the Employer, the dismissal was with just cause.
- The Arbitrator is not to apply the doctrines of either near cause or ball park justice.

SELECTING AN ARBITRATOR

The Arbitrator shall be   . However, if she is unable to accept the appointment, the parties agree to   as the Arbitrator.

– or –

The parties shall endeavour to agree upon an Arbitrator within 30 days of the date upon which this Agreement is signed. If no such Agreement is forthcoming, either party may apply under s. 10 of the *Arbitration Act, 1991* for the Court to select an Arbitrator.

TIME AND LOCATION OF THE ARBITRATION HEARING

The Arbitration hearing shall take place in the City of Toronto, at a location to be selected by the Arbitrator.

The Arbitration shall be held on the following dates:

– or –

The Arbitrator shall set the dates for the hearing after consultation with the parties.

PLEADINGS

The parties agree to not have pleadings of any sort.

– or –

The parties agree to not have pleadings as described in the Rules, but do agree to exchange written statements which indicate their positions, the points at issue, and the relief sought. These statements are to be exchanged by September 25, 1992.

– or –

The parties agree to exchange pleadings in accordance with Rules 25, 26, 27 and 28. The pleadings shall be filed with the Arbitrator rather than the Court.

– or –

The parties agree to exchange pleadings in accordance with Rules 25, 26, 27 and 28, subject to the following provision:

- The period for service for all pleadings shall be 10 days.

– or –

The parties agree that the pleadings already exchanged shall be used in the Arbitration.

DOCUMENTS

The parties agree that Rule 30 shall apply.

– or –

The parties agree to exchange copies of all documents they wish to rely upon at the Arbitration no later than 30 days prior to the Arbitration hearing. Documents not produced within that time frame may only be used at the Arbitration hearing with leave of the Arbitrator.

– or –

The parties agree that neither party will exchange documents or be obligated to advise the other party as to what documents it intends to rely upon at the Arbitration hearing.

– or –

The parties agree that Rule 30 shall apply subject to the following provision:

- Unless one party specifically requests the other party to produce the original of a document, each party may use photocopies.

MOTIONS AND INTERIM MATTERS

The parties agree that Rules 37 and 39 apply except that all Motions shall be heard at a location selected by the Arbitrator.

– or –

The parties agree that the Arbitrator shall rule on all procedural matters arising before the first hearing date. The Arbitrator shall set the procedure for the resolution of these matters.

– or –

The parties agree that the Arbitrator shall rule on all procedural matters arising before the first hearing date. All such matters shall be submitted to the Arbitrator in writing. The Arbitrator shall provide a brief written award within 10 days of receipt of the parties' submissions. No hearing on these matters shall be permitted unless specifically requested by the Arbitrator.

EXAMINATIONS FOR DISCOVERY

The parties agree to not have examinations for discovery.

– or –

The parties agree to have examinations for discovery in accordance with Rules 31, 32, 33, 34, 35 and 36.

– or –

The parties agree to have examinations for discovery in accordance with Rules 31, 32, 33, 34, 35 and 36, subject to the following provisions:

- The discoveries shall be held in Toronto on October 15 and 16, 1992.
- Each party is to be entitled to a maximum of 5 hours to conduct its discovery.

– or –

The parties agree that the examinations for discovery already held can be used in the Arbitration.

EVIDENCE AT THE ARBITRATION HEARING

The Arbitrator shall apply the laws of evidence as if the hearing was a trial in the Ontario Superior Court of Justice, including the provisions of Rule 53.

– or –

The Arbitrator shall apply the laws of evidence as if the hearing was a trial in the Ontario Superior Court of Justice, subject to the following provisions:

- The hearsay rule shall be applied as if the hearing was a labour arbitration under the *Labour Relations Act, 1995*.
- The parties may rely on photocopies of originals.
- No notice under the *Evidence Act*, R.S.O. 1990, c. E.23, is required for business records.

- All expert reports shall be served on the other party at least 30 days prior to the date of the hearing.

– or –

The parties shall not be permitted to present oral evidence. Rather, they are restricted to presenting the following evidence:

- documents;
- expert reports;
- transcripts of examinations;
- witness statements.

The parties are entitled to use the provisions of Rule 51 (Admissions).

REMEDIAL POWERS OF THE ARBITRATOR

The Arbitrator shall have all the remedial powers of a trial judge of the Ontario Superior Court of Justice.

– or –

The Arbitrator shall be limited in his remedial powers to:

- awarding monetary damages for lost income and benefits during the appropriate notice period;
- awarding damages for mental distress to a maximum of $5,000;
- awarding punitive damages to a maximum of $10,000;
- awarding prejudgment interest.

OFFERS TO SETTLE

Rule 49 applies to these proceedings.

– or –

Rule 49 applies to these proceedings, subject to the following provision:

- For an offer to be operative, it must be served on the other party within 20 days of the first hearing date.

REASONS OF THE ARBITRATOR

The Arbitrator is to give written reasons in his award.

– or –

The Arbitrator is not to give written reasons in his award.

AWARD OF COSTS

The Arbitrator shall have no power to award costs.

– or –

The Arbitrator shall have all the power of a judge of the Ontario Superior Court of Justice to award costs, including determination of the quantum.

– or –

The Arbitrator shall have all the power of a judge of the Ontario Superior Court of Justice to award costs, including determination of the quantum, subject to the following provisions:

- The Arbitrator may order one party to reimburse the other party, either in whole or in part, for its share of the Arbitrator's fees and disbursements.
- The maximum counsel fee at hearing shall be $1,500 per full day of the hearing.

FEES OF THE ARBITRATOR

The parties agree to share equally the fees and disbursements of the Arbitrator, and they agree that this responsibility shall not be the subject of any order for legal costs which the Arbitrator may award.

– or –

The parties acknowledge that each of them is directly liable to the Arbitrator to pay one-half of his fees and disbursements. However, the Arbitrator may, in his award of costs, order one party to reimburse the other party for part or all of that party's share of the fees and disbursements of the Arbitrator.

TRANSCRIPTS OF THE HEARING

The evidence at the arbitration hearing is to be transcribed.

– or –

The evidence at the arbitration hearing is not to be transcribed.

RIGHTS OF APPEAL

The parties agree that the decision of the Arbitrator is final and binding upon the parties, and no appeal to a Court is allowed.

– or –

The parties agree that an appeal from the Arbitrator's award is allowed only on a question of law.

– or –

The parties agree that an appeal from the Arbitrator's award is allowed only on a question of law or of mixed law and fact.

– or –

The parties agree that an appeal from the Arbitrator's award is allowed on a question of fact and/or law.

Existing Litigation

The parties agree to staying the present proceeding in the Ontario Superior Court of Justice until the Arbitration award is issued. At that time, the Arbitration award shall become a consent judgment in the court action.

– or –

The parties agree to discontinue the present proceedings in the Ontario Superior Court of Justice pursuant to Rule 23.01(c).

Confidentiality

The parties agree to keep the outcome of these arbitration proceedings strictly confidential, except as it may be necessary to implement or enforce the Arbitrator's award.

The parties agree that the Arbitration proceedings shall not be open to the public or the media.

Dated this   day of   , 2000

Insured   Insurer

_____   _____
Counsel for the Plaintiff   Counsel for the Defendant

Appendix 5.4
Sample Arbitration Agreement

MEDIATED SOLUTIONS INCORPORATED

415 Yonge Street, Suite 1802
Toronto, Ontario, Canada M5B 2E7
(416) 408-1700

AGREEMENT TO ARBITRATE

1. SCHEDULED DATE:

2. PARTIES:

Mediated Solutions Incorporated, 415 Yonge Street, Suite 1802, Toronto, Ontario M5B 2E7, (416) 408-1700, and these parties:

agree to arbitrate certain differences with **Judith H. Clarkson, R.N., B.A., LL.B.** as arbitrator. See the attached "Terms of Arbitration".

3. ISSUES:

The issues to be arbitrated are as follows:

4. COSTS OF THE ARBITRATION:

The fees are set out in Schedule "A". The parties agree to share equally the fees and any expenses related to the arbitration, but shall be jointly and severally responsible to Mediated Solutions Incorporated for any unpaid or outstanding fees and expenses. The parties shall each bear their own legal expenses.

5. SIGNING INDIVIDUALLY:

Each party may sign a separate copy of this agreement which, when so signed and delivered, shall be an original copy even though not signed by the other parties. All such separately signed copies shall together constitute evidence of all parties' consent to be bound by this agreement.

6. CONSENT TO THIS AGREEMENT:

Each of us has read this agreement and agrees to proceed with the arbitration on the terms contained in it.

Party: _____   Party: _____

Date: _____   Date: _____

Mediated Solutions Incorporated

Per: _____

Date: _____

Schedule "A"

FEE SCHEDULE

Arbitrator's Fee:	$250 per hour, plus GST.
Estimated Time Required:	_____ days/hours for hearing and reasons, not to be exceeded without the prior consent of the parties.

Disbursements:	Boardroom: $200 plus GST Other: At cost
Retainer:	Estimated fees for hearing and reasons, plus applicable GST, payable to Mediated Solutions Incorporated in advance of the hearing.
Cancellation Policy:	One (1) business day before the scheduled date: Full estimated fee. Two (2) to five (5) business days before scheduled date: One-half the estimated fee. Over five (5) business days before the scheduled date: $250.

MEDIATED SOLUTIONS INCORPORATED

415 Yonge Street, Suite 1802
Toronto, Ontario, Canada M5B 2E7
(416) 408-1700

TERMS OF ARBITRATION

1. In this arbitration,   shall be the claimant and   shall be the respondent.

2. The hearing will take place as follows unless otherwise agreed:

    Date:

    Time:

    Place:

3. The hearing shall be held in private and, unless the parties otherwise consent, only the parties, their lawyers (if any) and witnesses may be present.

4. The arbitrator shall decide the dispute in accordance with the law of Ontario, including equity.

5. The arbitrator shall render her award, including reasons, in writing not later than thirty (30) days after the last hearing day, and the award shall be released when the arbitrator's fees and expenses have been paid in full.

6. There shall be no appeal, whether on a question of law, fact or mixed fact and law.

7. Other than what is specified in these terms, the procedures governing this arbitration shall be determined by the arbitrator in her sole discretion.

8. The parties will conduct themselves in good faith throughout the arbitration. The parties shall provide full disclosure to each other of all necessary information in order to enable the opposite party to know the case it has to meet. To this end, each party will deliver to the other and file with the arbitrator fifteen (15) days before the date set for the hearing:

   (a) a written statement indicating the points in issue, the facts supporting the party's position, and the relief sought;

   (b) copies of all documents (including expert opinions) and other materials of any kind upon which the party intends to rely for any purpose at the hearing; and

   (c) the names and addresses of any witnesses the party proposes to call and a summary of their proposed testimony.

   Failing this, no issue or claim for relief may be raised, no document or material of any kind may be tendered or relied on, and no witness may be called to testify without the consent of the opposite party or the permission of the arbitrator.

9. Where possible, the parties will deliver to the arbitrator an agreed statement of facts and/or law fifteen (15) days before the date of the hearing.

10. The parties may apply to the arbitrator for any further production or for the examination of any party on oath or affirmation with respect to the dispute, as the arbitrator in her sole discretion sees fit.

11. The arbitration is a confidential process. The parties and the arbitrator agree to keep all communications and information disclosed during the arbitration in confidence, except that the arbitrator may make disclosure:

   (a) for research or educational purposes, on an anonymous basis;

   (b) where ordered to do so by a judicial authority or where required to do so by law; or

   (c) where the information suggests an actual or potential threat to human life or safety.

12. The parties will not initiate or take any fresh steps in any legal proceedings related to the issues in this arbitration while the arbitration is in progress.

Part C

Other ADR Applications

Drafting ADR Clauses

Key Concepts

- Increasingly, insurance companies are including comprehensive dispute resolution clauses in their contracts and policies in order to expedite constructive and early resolution of any disputes.

- Dispute resolution clauses should not be inserted as boilerplate, but should be drafted to specifically address the parties' needs.

- ADR clauses typically include provisions for negotiation, mediation, and/or a final binding arbitration.

- Three objectives of a dispute resolution position should be: speed of disposition, certainty of process, and certainty of result.

- A multi-step dispute resolution clause, developed in the United States, is used by many organizations.

- Arbitration provisions should include the following elements: time lines, jurisdiction, certainty regarding the arbitrator's procedure, finality of the award, confidentiality, and a provision avoiding protracted interlocutory steps.

- Dispute resolution clauses should be drafted clearly and simply in order to avoid difficulties in interpretation and application which may lead to additional conflict and delay.

- Optimally, any dispute resolution clause should address the following areas: time limits; enforceability; selection of the neutral; confidentiality; disclosure and discovery of documents; and applicability of existing procedures and/or legislation.

1. INTRODUCTION

Advocates in the insurance industry may be called upon from time to time to consult or advise with regard to, or to implement, an existing dispute resolution clause. This chapter provides a brief overview of the types of clauses which are available, and it gives suggestions for drafting them. Given that many legal writers have advocated against using boilerplate in this particular situation, there are a limited number of examples included in this chapter. However, further examples of types of clauses can be obtained from the reference list in Appendix 6.1 at the end of this chapter.

When parties first negotiate business or insurance arrangements, they should at the same time negotiate an agreement as to how disputes will be resolved. It is much more difficult to reach agreement on dispute resolution after a conflict has arisen.

Generally, three steps are considered in dispute resolution clauses:

(1) direct negotiation between the parties;
(2) some other form of non-binding resolution such as mediation; and
(3) a binding form of resolution such as arbitration.

These concepts are discussed at length in Chapters 3 through 5, and that discussion will not be repeated here. However, one hybrid has been recommended by a well-known U.S. dispute resolution organization, which should be discussed. This is the multi-step provision recommended by the CPR Institute.[1] The CPR Institute suggests including the following three successive stages of dispute resolution in any business agreement:

(1) *negotiation:* a provision requiring negotiations between executives with decision-making authority who are at a higher level than the personnel involved in the dispute;
(2) *non-binding resolution:* a provision requiring some form of non-binding dispute resolution such as mediation or a mini-trial;
(3) *binding resolution:* a "back stop" final adjudication device such as binding arbitration or, if no other procedure is agreed upon, litigation.

2. CONSIDERATIONS WHEN DRAFTING A DISPUTE RESOLUTION CLAUSE

Advocates who have been asked to draft provisions for dispute resolution should consider the following twelve areas. These are also included in a dispute resolution clause checklist in Appendix 6.1 at the end of the chapter.

---

[1] CPR Institute for Dispute Resolution, http://www.cpradr.org. Click "Procedures & Clauses", then "ADR Clauses – US/Canada", then "Abbreviated Clauses for Standard Business Agreements".

Designated intervenor: Very often, dispute resolution clauses indicate that any intervenors may be used provided all parties involved are in unanimous agreement. If the parties cannot agree on a designated intervenor, it is useful to indicate the source from which the intervenor or neutral dispute resolution practitioner will be drawn. Very often, specific organizations will be included as a source of qualified, competent, experienced neutrals, and a process will be designated for assigning or arbitrarily selecting one of those neutrals. Some of the organizations which typically provide neutrals in these situations are listed in Appendix 1.6.

Cost: It is important, in drafting a dispute resolution clause, to consider who will pay for the intervenor. Will the parties split the cost evenly, or will the institutional party pay the full amount? If payment is not prescribed, the matter is purely at the discretion of the person drafting the clause and/or can be a negotiable item. Dispute clauses should specify that the parties are responsible for the cost of their own legal representation, travel, etc.

Jurisdiction of the designated intervenor: Advocates should specify the mandate of the intervenor. For example, if the intervenor is a mediator, the clause could state that the mediator may only mediate particular types of disputes. In the case of an arbitrator, it is even more important to clarify the intended jurisdiction.

Procedural considerations such as time lines and notice: The advocate drafting dispute resolution clauses should give some consideration to the optimal time lines for any of the previously described steps. For example, it may be important to an insurer that identification of the dispute and referral to some sort of direct negotiation be implemented within a particular period of time. Requirements for notice should also be carefully specified. These time frames can vary from five days to three months. It is not the author's intent to prescribe time limits, but to highlight the need for the drafter to pay attention to the parties' needs in this regard. Another reason for clarity is to limit ambiguity as to when various steps in the dispute resolution process will occur.

Disclosure and exchange of information: As part of any fair process, there should be provision for exchanging relevant information and documents in a timely fashion. Once again, the type of dispute and the type of intervention prescribed will inform the specificity regarding that exchange. Some negotiation clauses have specified wording such as the following:

> Any party may give the other party written notice of any dispute not resolved in the normal course of business. Within [15] days after delivery of the notice, the receiving party shall submit to the other a written response. The notice and the response shall include (a) a statement of each party's position and a summary of arguments supporting that position, and (b) the name and title of the executive who will represent that party and of any other person who will accompany the executive.[2]

---

[2] CPR Institute for Dispute Resolution, http://www.cpradr.org. Click "Procedures & Clauses", then "ADR Clauses – US/Canada", then "Detailed ADR Clauses for Business Agreements".

In the case of arbitration, the process of disclosure and providing discovery of documents may need to be very detailed. Once again, when drafting this clause, consideration should be given to the intention of the parties involved.

Confidentiality provision: A hallmark of mediation and private arbitration is the ability to prescribe the terms and conditions of confidentiality. Consideration should be given to including in the clause some directive setting out the mutual expectations of confidentiality. For example, one dispute resolution clause states:

> All negotiations pursuant to this clause are confidential and shall be treated as compromise and settlement negotiations for purposes of applicable rules of evidence.[3]

Location: In the case of national or international disputes, it is particularly important to set out the location for the dispute resolution and/or a means for fairly deciding the location. If the dispute is across borders, this may be a point of contention. If the clause has the potential to involve institutional clients and individual claimants, some consideration may need to be given to travel costs and the availability of facilities and intervenors.

Applicable/governing law: There are statutes in Canada and in the U.S. which govern arbitration: see the list in Appendix 5.1 for the Canadian legislation. It is important to consider whether there needs to be a dispute resolution clause setting out which statutes govern in a particular dispute, particularly in the case of arbitration. For example, one arbitration clause states:

> The arbitration shall be governed by the *Federal Arbitration Act*, 9 U.S.C. §§1-16 and judgment upon the award rendered by the arbitrator(s) may be entered by any court having jurisdiction thereof. The place of the arbitration shall be _____ . [The arbitrator(s) are not empowered to award damages in excess of compensatory damages.][4]

Immunity and compellability of the designated intervenor: Drafters of dispute resolution clauses may wish to consider building in an immunity for mediators operating under the clause. This area may be considered in conjunction with confidentiality provisions to ensure that "without prejudice" discussions are not disclosed in a court of law.

Enforceability: There may be legal concerns about the enforceability of any given dispute resolution clause. It has been identified that properly drafted arbitration agreements are generally enforceable in U.S. courts and in the courts of other industrial nations.[5] It is generally viewed that agreements to mediate between responsible companies or individuals should carry considerable weight and will substantially increase the likelihood of a consensus-based resolution. The enforceability of such resolution clauses is a matter of law, including the law

---

[3] *Ibid.*

[4] *Ibid.*

[5] CPR Institute for Dispute Resolution, http://www.cpradr.org. Click "Procedures & Clauses", then "ADR Clauses – US/Canada", then "Legal Concerns".

of contract and any pertinent statutes.[6] It is critical to appreciate that dispute resolution choices to which organizations privately agree, or as articulated in policies or commercial documents, can be enforced by the courts.[7] A multi-step dispute resolution clause, developed in the United States, and used by many organizations, guides the parties gradually from consensus-based to binding processes. This is an attempt to give the parties flexibility in determining the correct process for a given dispute. Rather than attempting to force a process on the parties, this clause sets the stage for the disputing parties and their advisors to consider an array of options other than traditional litigation.[8]

Representation of the disputants: This is a self-descriptive area indicating that the disputants are responsible for their own representation and/or that the disputants are expected to participate without representation. In either case, it is important to set out the expectations with regard to who will participate and who will pay for representatives to participate. One pitfall is the disputant who brings along an accounting expert, legal counsel, an engineering expert, and a structured settlement expert. There may be reason to place some limitations on who may participate in the process.

Authority to settle: Particularly in the case of negotiation and mediation, all parties need to have a clear understanding and be of a common mind that the desired outcome is resolution. Drafters of dispute resolution clauses should consider whether it is desirable to have full settlement authority present at the mediation. The different types of authority have been described as legal, advisory, conditional and *de facto* authority.[9] Legal authority has to do with the proper legal parties. This is particularly important in the case of corporate entities. Advisory authority is the ability to obtain input, particularly during the option generation stage and during finalization of any settlement agreement. Conditional authority refers to the situation where the approval of a third party not directly involved in the dispute may be required as a condition of settlement. This is quite common in the insurance sector where the spokesperson at the table may need approval from someone at a higher level. *De facto* authority includes those who may influence the parties at the table. It is an informal type of control which may not have a basis in law, but can influence the negotiation and mediation process as much as more formal types of authority. Given these different types of authority and the potentially different perceptions of parties, it is imperative that the drafter of the pertinent clause consider the type of authority required in the given situation.

---

[6] Genevieve A. Chornenki, *The Corporate Counsel Guide to Dispute Resolution* (Aurora, Ontario: Canada Law Book Inc., 1999), p. 186.

[7] *Supra.*

[8] Richard Jackman, "Multi-Step: The Next Generation DR Clause", *ADR Forum* (CCH Canada Ltd., January 1995).

[9] Richard J. Weiler, "Authority to Settle at Mediation", *Alternative Dispute Resolution Practice Manual* (CCH Canada Ltd., 1998).

3. THE MULTI-STEP DISPUTE RESOLUTION CLAUSE

A hybrid form of dispute resolution clause, called the multi-step dispute resolution clause, has been recommended by a well-known U.S. dispute resolution organization as well as by the CPR Institute.

(a) Examples

Three Canadian examples of multi-step dispute resolution clauses are:

(1) Multi-Step Short Form;
(2) Multi-Step Clause with Mediation Specified; and
(3) Multi-Step Long Form.

(b) Multi-Step Short Form[10]

(i) *Clause*

If a dispute arises between the parties relating to this Agreement, the parties agree to use the following procedure prior to either party pursuing other available remedies:

(a) A meeting shall be held promptly between the parties, attended by individuals with decision-making authority regarding the dispute, to attempt in good faith to negotiate a resolution of the dispute.

(b) If, within [30] days after such meeting, the parties have not succeeded in negotiating a resolution of the dispute, they will jointly appoint a mutually acceptable neutral person not affiliated with either of the parties (the "neutral"), seeking assistance in such regard from [named organization] if they have been unable to agree upon such appointment within [40] days from the initial meeting. The fees of the neutral shall be shared equally by the parties.

(c) In consultation with the neutral, the parties will select or devise an alternative dispute resolution procedure ("ADR") by which they will attempt to resolve the dispute, at a time and place for the ADR to be held, with the neutral making the decision as to the procedure and/or place and time (but unless circumstances require otherwise, not later than [60] days after selection of the neutral) if the parties have been unable to agree on any such matters within [20] days after initial consultation with the neutral.

(d) The parties agree to participate in good faith in the ADR to its conclusion as designated by the neutral. If the parties are not successful in resolving the dispute through ADR, then the parties:

[Drafter may select one of the following alternatives to provide for some other means of obtaining a binding and final resolution.]

---

[10] G.A. Chornenki, *op. cit.*, footnote 6, p. 201. Reproduced with permission of Richard J. Weiler, C.Med.

   (i) [May agree to submit the matter to binding arbitration or a private adjudicator, or either party may seek an adjudicated resolution through the appropriate court.]

  (ii) [Agree that the dispute shall be settled by arbitration in accordance with the Arbitration Rules of the Arbitration and Mediation Institute of Ontario Inc. and judgment upon the award rendered by the arbitrator(s) may be entered in any court having jurisdiction.]

 (iii) [Agree that either party may initiate litigation upon [7] days' written notice to the other party.]

(ii) *Structure of the Multi-Step Short Form*[11]

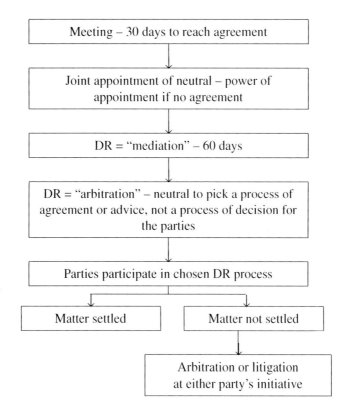

---

[11] *Ibid.*, p. 200.

(c) Multi-Step with Mediation Specified[12]

(i) *Clause*

If a dispute arises between the parties relating to this Agreement, the parties agree to use the following procedure prior to either party pursuing other available remedies:

(a) A meeting shall be held promptly between the parties, attended by individuals with decision-making authority regarding the dispute, to attempt in good faith to negotiate a resolution of the dispute.

(b) If, within [30] days after such meeting, the parties have not succeeded in negotiating a resolution of the dispute, they will jointly appoint a mutually acceptable neutral person not affiliated with either of the parties (the "neutral"), seeking assistance in such regard from [named organization] if they have been unable to agree upon such appointment within [40] days from the initial meeting. The fees of the neutral shall be shared equally by the parties.

(c) In consultation with the neutral, the parties will select or devise an alternative dispute resolution procedure ("ADR") by which they will attempt to resolve the dispute, at a time and place for the ADR to be held, with the neutral making the decision as to the procedure, and/or place and time (but unless circumstances require otherwise, not later than [60] days after selection of the neutral) if the parties have been unable to agree on any such matters within [20] days after initial consultation with the neutral.

(d) The parties agree to participate in good faith in the ADR to its conclusion as designated by the neutral. If the parties are not successful in resolving the dispute through ADR, then the parties:

[Drafter may select one of the following alternatives to provide for some other means of obtaining a binding and final resolution.]

(i) [May agree to submit the matter to binding arbitration or a private adjudicator, or either party may seek an adjudicated resolution through the appropriate court.]

(ii) [Agree that the dispute shall be settled by arbitration in accordance with the Arbitration Rules of the Arbitration and Mediation Institute of Ontario Inc. and judgment upon the award rendered by the arbitrator(s) may be entered in any court having jurisdiction.]

(iii) [Agree that either party may initiate litigation upon [7] days' written notice to the other party.]

---

[12] *Ibid.*, pp. 202-203. Reproduced with permission of Richard J. Weiler, C.Med.

(ii) *Structure of the Multi-Step with Mediation Specified*[13]

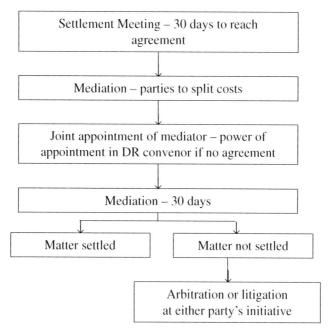

(d) Multi-Step Long Form[14]

(i) *Clause*

(a) <u>Agreement to Use Procedure</u> In the event of a dispute between the parties arising out of or related to this Agreement (the "dispute"), the parties agree to utilize the procedures specified in this section (the "procedure"), unless otherwise modified by written agreement of the parties at the time the dispute arises.

(b) <u>Initiation of Procedure</u> A party seeking to initiate the procedure (the "initiating party") shall give written notice to the other party, describing briefly the nature of the dispute and its claim and identifying an individual with authority to settle the dispute on its behalf. The party receiving such notice ("responding party") shall have [5] days within which to designate, in a written notice given to the initiating party, an individual with authority to settle the dispute on its behalf. (The individuals so designated shall be known as the "authorized individuals".) [Absent agreement by the parties, neither of the authorized individuals shall have had direct substandard involvement in the matters involved in the dispute.]

---

[13] *Ibid.*, p. 202.
[14] *Ibid.*, pp. 205-207. Reproduced with permission of Richard J. Weiler, C.Med.

(c) <u>Unassisted Settlement</u> The authorized individuals shall make such investigation as they deem appropriate and thereafter promptly (but in no event later than [30] days from the date of the initiating parties' notice) shall commence discussions concerning resolution of the dispute. If the dispute has not been resolved within [30] days from the commencement of discussions (such [30th] day being the "submission date"), it shall be submitted to alternative dispute resolution ("ADR") in accordance with the following procedure.

(d) <u>Selection of Neutral</u> The parties shall have [10] days from the submission date to agree upon a mutually acceptable neutral person not affiliated with either of the parties (the "neutral"). If no neutral has been selected within such time, the parties agree jointly to request [named Organization] and/or another mutually agreed upon provider of neutral services to supply within [10] days a list of potential neutrals with qualifications as specified by the parties in the joint request. Within [5] days of receipt of the list, the parties shall independently rank the proposed candidates, shall simultaneously exchange rankings, and shall select as the neutral the individual receiving the highest combined ranking who is available to serve.

(e) <u>Time and Place for ADR</u> In consultation with the neutral, the parties shall promptly designate a mutually convenient time and place for the ADR (and unless circumstances require otherwise, such time to be not later than [45] days after selection of the neutral).

(f) <u>Exchange of Information</u> In the event either of the parties has substantial need for information in the possession of the other party in order to prepare for the ADR, the parties shall attempt in good faith to agree on procedures for the expeditious exchange of such information, with the help of the neutral if required.

(g) <u>Summary of Views</u> One week prior to the first scheduled session of the ADR, each party shall deliver to the neutral and to the other party a concise written summary of its views on the matter in dispute.

(h) <u>Staffing the ADR</u> In the ADR, each party shall be represented by the authorized individual and by counsel. In addition, each party may bring such additional persons as needed to respond to questions, contribute information and participate in the negotiations, the number of such additional persons to be agreed upon by the parties in advance, with the assistance of the neutral, if necessary.

(i) <u>Conduct of ADR</u> The parties, in consultation with the neutral, will agree upon a format for the meetings, designed to ensure that both the neutral and authorized individuals have an opportunity to hear an oral presentation of each party's views on the matter in dispute, and that the authorized parties attempt a negotiated resolution of the matter in dispute, with or without the assistance of counsel or others, but with the assistance of the neutral. To this end, the neutral is authorized to conduct both joint meetings and separate private caucuses with the parties. The neutral will keep confidential all information learned in private caucus with either party unless specifically authorized by such party to make disclosure of the information to the other party.

(j) The Neutral's Views The neutral (i) shall, unless requested not to do so by both parties, provide his opinion to both parties on the probable outcome should the matter be litigated, and (ii) shall, if requested to do so by both parties, make one or more recommendations as to the terms of a possible settlement, upon any conditions imposed by the parties (including, but not limited to, a minimum and maximum amount). The neutral shall base his opinions [and recommendations] on information being available to both parties, excluding such information as may be disclosed to him by the parties in confidence. The opinions and recommendations of the neutral shall not be binding on the parties.

(k) Termination of Procedure The parties agree to participate in the ADR procedure to its conclusion (as designated by the neutral) and not to terminate negotiations concerning resolution of the matters in dispute until at least [10] days thereafter. Each party agrees not to commence a lawsuit or seek other remedies prior to the conclusion of the [10]-day post-ADR negotiation; provided, however, that either party may commence litigation within [5] days prior to the date after which the commencement of litigation could be barred by the applicable statute of limitations or in order to request an injunction to prevent irreparable harm, in which event, the parties agree (except as prohibited by court order) to nevertheless continue to participate in the ADR to its conclusion.

(l) Fees of Neutral; Disqualification The fees of the neutral shall be shared equally by the parties. The neutral shall be disqualified as a witness, consultant, expert or counsel for either party with respect to the matters in dispute and any related matters.

(m) Confidentiality The ADR procedure is confidential, and no stenographic, visual or audio record shall be made. All conduct, statements, promises, offers, views and opinions, whether oral or written, made in the course of the ADR by either of the parties, their agents, employees, representatives or other invitees by the neutral (who will be the parties' joint agent for the purposes of these compromise negotiations) are confidential. Such conduct, statements, promises, offers, views and opinions shall not be discoverable or admissible for any purposes, including impeachment, in any litigation or other proceedings involving the parties, and shall be disclosed to no one, not an agent, employee, expert, witness or representative of either party; provided, however, that evidence otherwise discoverable or admissible is not excluded from discovery ordination as a result of its use in the ADR.

(ii) *Structure of the Multi-Step Long Form*[15]

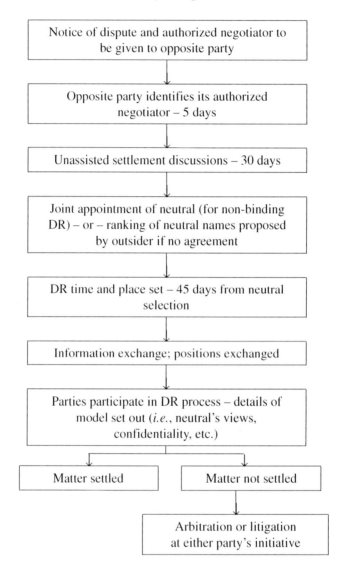

Summary

Ideally, ADR clauses should be constructed simply and clearly to address the specific needs of the parties. The clauses should address time limits, enforceability, selection of a neutral, disclosure and discovery of documents, applicable legislation, and confidentiality.

APPENDIX 6.1[16]
CHECKLIST OF DISPUTE RESOLUTION CLAUSES

☐ Designated intervenor
☐ Cost
☐ Jurisdiction of the designated intervenor
☐ Procedural considerations such as time lines and notice
☐ Disclosure and exchange of information
☐ Confidentiality provision
☐ Location
☐ Applicable/governing law
☐ Immunity and compellability of the designated intervenor
☐ Enforceability
☐ Representation of the disputants
☐ Authority to settle

---

[16] For a discussion on these points, see pp. 145-7.

Designing ADR Processes

Key Concepts

- Advocates in the insurance context play a role in designing ADR processes by identifying the need, by participating as part of the design team, by acting as intervenors or advocates within the system, and by defending the system should it come under scrutiny.

- The design of an ADR system should take into consideration the following principles:
  - compliance with organizational values;
  - compliance with contractual and statutory obligations;
  - education and guidance for stakeholders;
  - use of a fair and open process;
  - efficient fulfilment of the mandate within budgetary constraints;
  - provision of adequate and cost-effective screening of complaints;
  - resolution of "minor" complaints swiftly and completely;
  - management of third party interventions and resolution;
  - initiation of fair and competent investigations where necessary.

- There are four generic steps to designing an ADR system: diagnosis, design, implementation, and monitoring and evaluation.

- The goals of an ADR system determine its design.

- ADR systems in the insurance context serve in-house purposes, aid in dealing with external/customer complaints, and/or facilitate the case-specific handling of special classes of claimants.

1. INTRODUCTION

One trend in the insurance context which has been identified in recent years is the increasing institutionalization of ADR processes. As has been discussed in previous chapters, mediation has become mandated in the court context, different forms of ADR have been implemented and mandated by statute in various insurance commissions across Canada, and other kinds of informal ADR processes are being used in the regulatory context. It is beyond the scope of this book to provide a comprehensive overview of all the theory and principles incorporated into dispute system design. This chapter will endeavour instead to give ADR advocates an overview of the general steps to be considered in designing an ADR process. It will discuss four generic design steps and will apply them to two classic insurance situations, the in-house case management/ADR screening tool, and the design of an ad hoc dispute resolution system to handle a special class of claimants. The chapter will close with a commentary on the role of the advocate in designing a dispute resolution system.

2. INSTITUTIONALIZATION OF ADR

Some authors have observed that, in designing dispute resolution guidelines, model procedures and protocols for government bodies or private sector insurers, efforts have tended to be focused on the following four areas:[1]

(1) identifying cases for ADR;
(2) specifying the ADR process;
(3) structuring the process; and
(4) selecting the intervenor.

Identifying cases for ADR: It has been noted that the three indicators most frequently used to select cases are the dollar amount in controversy, the nature of the dispute, and the relationship of the parties. A detailed discussion of the criteria commonly used to screen cases for ADR in the insurance context is included at pp. 11-14.

Specifying the ADR process: It has been observed by the author that facilitative mediation is increasingly becoming a first choice of individuals and organizations, followed by another ADR process such as arbitration if necessary.

Structuring the process: Many systems provide specific guidelines for structuring the procedural steps. These include detailed rules for arbitration and comprehensive guidelines for conducting other kinds of procedures in complex cases. Examples of the areas relevant to mediation and arbitration are included on pp. 70-72 and 113-20, while a commentary on the use of multi-step dispute resolution clauses is included on pp. 148-54.

---

[1] H.N. Mazadoorian, "Institutionalizing ADR: Few Risks, Many Benefits" (April 1994), 12:4 CPR's Alternatives III-10.

Selecting the neutral: Some procedures select neutrals for the disputants, while others allow varying levels of disputant input into the selection process. Most commonly, the parties choose from a short list provided by the sponsoring or administering ADR organization.

3. PRINCIPLES OF DISPUTE SYSTEM DESIGN

Authors C.A. Costantino and C.S. Merchant identify six principles of dispute system design:[2]

(1) Put the focus on the underlying needs and concerns of the disputants by encouraging the use of interest-based methods such as negotiation and mediation.

(2) Provide "loopbacks" or procedures that allow the disputants to return to a lower cost method such as negotiation.

(3) Provide low-cost rights and power "back-ups". This can be accomplished by offering potentially lowest-cost alternatives[3] such as arbitration if interest-based procedures fail.

(4) Build in "consultation before" and "feedback after" design completion. This can be achieved by notifying and consulting with the relevant stakeholders prior to taking any action, and by providing post-dispute feedback to prevent similar disputes in the future.

(5) Arrange the procedures in a low-to-high-cost sequence. Advocates can accomplish this by encouraging negotiation before mediation, mediation prior to arbitration, and so on.

(6) Provide the motivation, skills and resources necessary to make the dispute resolution design a success. It is imperative that ADR procedures be supported by promotion, training and financing so they can be used to their full potential.

4. STAGES OF DISPUTE RESOLUTION SYSTEM DESIGN

Four generic stages of dispute resolution system design are diagnosis, design, implementation and evaluation.[4]

Diagnosis: The diagnosis stage of an ADR system design should include a needs and conflict analysis, including data collection. This may be conducted with the assistance of internal and external consultation. The data collected should review:

---

[2] C.A. Costantino and C.S. Merchant, *Designing Conflict Management Systems: A Guide to Creating Productive and Healthy Organizations* (San Francisco: Jossey-Bass Publishers, 1996).
[3] It should be noted that arbitration and other forms of dispute resolution are not necessarily low-cost.
[4] Costantino and Merchant, *op. cit.*, footnote 2.

- the system currently in place;
- the type and number of disputes;
- the parties to the dispute; and/or
- baseline costs.

A needs and conflict analysis should identify the strengths and weaknesses of existing systems and processes, both formal and informal. Consultation with the appropriate stakeholders at this stage is imperative. For example, in a review of the complaints and disciplines procedure for the regulatory body of one self-governing profession, members of the profession, members and staff of the governing body, members of the public, as well as lawyers who acted as prosecutors or defence counsel for the profession were included in the consultation.

Design: Design is the practical application of the conflict and needs analysis to organizational objectives. Early in the design stage, program goals should be identified. Typical program objectives include:

- reduction of costs, *e.g.*, settlement, legal, administrative costs;
- reduction of delay;
- maintenance of, or improvement in, disputant/client satisfaction;
- preservation of equity of outcomes;
- promotion of a less contentious environment; and
- satisfaction of the legal and cultural requirements of the organization.

Participant and case characteristics should be considered. Who are the disputants? How frequently does a dispute occur? Consider existing and desired program outcomes. Are the existing organizational goals and mission statements directly relevant? What are the causes of disputes? The existing transaction costs, satisfaction with outcomes, and dispute recurrences should be taken into consideration in the design. The current entry point to dispute resolution processes should also be considered, with a view to determining what other entry points need to be evaluated. Finally, the question should be asked: What dispute resolution options are available and/or desired?

Implementation: A successful implementation plan includes time frames and deadlines. The plan should clearly outline who will participate in screening, convening and intervening, and what education and training of the participants is required. The terms of intervention should also be set out in order to ensure a smooth transition and consistent application of the new rules and procedures.

Evaluation and modification: The evaluation and monitoring system should identify the party who will conduct the evaluation and the terms of reference. The evaluation should revisit program goals, collect the data needed to study and analyze the system, and develop appropriate measures of outcomes. Examples of outcome measurement could include program outcomes, participant and case characteristics, and program implementation characteristics. Pilot testing is well known in the insurance context and is a useful way to work out implementation bugs and provide feedback to users.[5]

---

[5] Frank Carr, "How to Design a Dispute Resolution Program" (March 1994), 12:3 CPR's Alternatives III-7.

(a) Benefits of Pilot Testing

The purpose of pilot testing is to observe the designed system under actual conditions before committing the organization fully to the ADR program. This step provides information about the effectiveness of the methods and procedures developed, and it gives the affected parties an opportunity to comment on their experiences.

Time period: A definite date should be set for the pilot testing to end and evaluation to begin.

Procedures: Participants in the pilot phase need to know precisely what is being tested. The purpose of pilot testing is to test procedures, not to develop them.

Site selection: A single site may be sufficient in some instances, while several sites may be necessary for larger organizations. The selected locations should have an adequate number of disputes to provide sufficient data to evaluate the ADR methods and procedures.

Local management support: ADR needs the support and commitment of the managers at the pilot sites. This includes senior managers who have to provide the resources as well as the managers who have to participate in good faith.

Training: Pilot testing provides an excellent opportunity for practising awareness and system training. Conducting training during the pilot testing will let the system designers know if the training is effective.

Technical assistance: Throughout the pilot testing, technical assistance needs to be provided by the system designer in order to clarify the ADR methods and procedures.

(b) Examples of ADR System Design

(i) *Case Scenario One*

Background: A large insurance company with an in-house legal department identified that one counsel sent no cases to mediation, while the other lawyers would send cases intermittently. In keeping with the size of the organization and the organization's corporate culture, which valued efficiency and systematic approaches to its use of resources, general counsel determined that there needed to be a more systematic and consistent approach to ADR referrals.

Identification of the problem: The job of determining organizational needs fell to the manager of the legal department. The manager reviewed the current situation and discovered that there was no system in place to govern referral to ADR. Rather, the choice was left to the discretion of the individual lawyers. The manager ascertained that hundreds of files were opened every year and that the in-house tracking system identified each case by name, type of issue, and counsel. Further, the system provided data such as the administrative and legal costs on any particular file. A further needs analysis showed that more statistical information could be gleaned from the system in order to determine baseline costs for average cases. However, there was no way of determining at what stage of the lawsuit any individual case was.

Retaining a dispute resolution expert: The manager decided that she did not have sufficient knowledge and expertise to design an appropriate system for this department, so she retained an outside dispute resolution consultant to take the lead on the remainder of the project. The consultant interviewed members of the legal department, administrative staff, and counsel in an effort to understand the organizational objectives in implementing some kind of ADR screening process. The consultant discovered that the organization was concerned with reducing costs and delay, wanted to improve client satisfaction, and sought more predictability in handling the organization's case load. The consultant also examined mission statements and annual reports, as well as the organizational culture.

Design phase: The consultant once again involved the administrative and legal staff in examining existing program outcomes and trying to identify patterns in the types of cases handled. It was determined that mediation was the process of choice because of its growing acceptance in the insurance industry and because all counsel in the department had experience as participants in various mediation forums. It was also identified that whatever system was put in place would have to be tested in order to determine if referral to ADR would save the company money. With the assistance of the staff, the consultant drafted a policy and an ADR screening tool which included consideration of the data already available through the organization's current system. A form was developed with a checklist for the lawyers to complete. The form also included spaces for the law clerks, in the course of their normal file workup, to insert certain pieces of information such as the stage of each lawsuit, the identity of opposing counsel, etc.

Implementation and pilot testing: Keeping the quarterly and yearly annual filing requirements for the organization in mind, an implementation plan was developed with time frames and deadlines. It was agreed that each counsel would use the screening tool to select a certain number of cases for referral to ADR, and that those interventions would be convened as per insurance industry business practices. An invitation to mediate would be sent out in writing, and then the actual scheduling of dates and arranging of venue would be arranged by the administrative support staff. Counsel's role was to suggest and start discussions to mutually agree on a mediator, and then to prepare for and attend the mediation.

Evaluation and fine-tuning: After six months, the pilot project statistics were evaluated against sample cases settled in the previous two years without ADR. The organization then had a baseline to determine whether administrative and legal costs were in fact less and whether the final settlement amount exceeded or was within the anticipated reserve set aside for the file. Once the pilot testing period was over, the external ADR consultant met again with the department, and together the policy was fine-tuned. A finalized format was shared with internal and external counsel.

(ii) *Case Scenario Two*

Background: An insurance company identified a finite group of claimants with an issue going back many years. The issue was a concern around the terms of a particular kind of policy and whether the complainants had been misled or not. Due to the mergers of various insurance companies, the liability for these claims was concentrated in a few large insurance companies, despite the fact that these insurers had not sold the original policy.

Identification of the problem: The need for an ad hoc ADR system was identified by counsel for the defendant insurance company, who determined that a more expedient, cost-effective way of settling claims would be beneficial. He also noted that whatever method was used to settle the claims had to be consistent and preserve equity of outcomes. He considered whether to work in house in putting together an alternative process for settling the files, or whether to farm out the design of the process to a recognized dispute resolution firm. Given the multiple nature of this class of disputes, the process would have to focus on expediency, exchange of sufficient information to ensure that the claimants and the insurer could make a useful decision, a formula for determining a payout that would preserve equity of outcomes, and an adjudicative or binding process for finality. Knowing that these kinds of claims often take place in the context of a class action lawsuit, the in-house counsel also anticipated that any ad hoc ADR system might need to be defended at a certification hearing before a judge. Once the system was designed and fine-tuned to meet the needs of the insurer, counsel would need to consider retaining an independent dispute resolution professional to evaluate the process. Implementation would most likely be delayed until the process had been reviewed by a judge at a certification hearing.

In the author's experience, the most likely criteria to be used by an independent ADR dispute resolution expert evaluating an ad hoc process would be:

(1) *Is the program procedurally fair?* To determine this, the expert would review the use of a third party arm's length neutral, the terms of any arbitration agreement and process, any formulas for determining payout, and any provision for mutual disclosure and informed consent.

(2) *Are the time lines expeditious and reasonable?* The expert would here consider the practicality of the policyholder fulfilling any of the given steps in the time allocated. A comparison with a baseline such as a similar program would be beneficial.

(3) *Is the process transparent?* With regard to transparency, the expert might review the brochure and definitions for clarity. Ideally, any brochures, forms or agreements should be clearly organized and written in plain English. A glossary might be included to reduce confusion. At the same time, there should be an opportunity to obtain independent legal advice should the policyholders decide they want representation as part of the process.

(4) *Is the outcome final?* Finality of the outcome is subject to statutory rights to seek judicial review. The expert might consider whether the ad hoc ADR

process is within the governing legislation and industry practice for that jurisdiction.

(5) *Are the costs of the program reasonable?* As costs are a tremendous incentive for institutions and individuals to participate in ADR programs, the reasonableness of the program cost would certainly be a ground for comparison. Accessibility of the program is one cost factor. For example, policyholders may choose to participate in any number of ways, such as by telephone, through written submissions, or in a face-to-face oral hearing. Limits on the geographic location may be a barrier to accessibility. Conditions for a fee refund might also be an area of consideration regarding reasonableness of the costs.

(c) The Role of Advocates in Designing Dispute Resolution Processes

ADR advocates, whether in-house or external, can play a role in designing dispute resolution processes. There are several different roles of the advocate.

Identifying the need for a dispute resolution system: Advocates are in a unique position to monitor and to provide objective insight into case load problems, particular types of issues, and classes of claimants. They may observe that a particular issue, although described as a difficulty convening, is really a difficulty selecting the optimal ADR process and the appropriate entry point in particular circumstances. In such a case, the advocate may suggest mediation by a third party mediator rather than pursuing expensive surveillance. When observed problems have a systemic component or arise on a regular basis, the organization may need to reassess its internal ADR systems and/or design, and implement new ones. In one case, an advocate identified a problem in dealing with disgruntled clients when it became apparent that lawsuits were being commenced to access information to which the clients were entitled by law. In that case, the advocate alerted the client organization to the need for a systematic method of providing this information and dealing expeditiously with client complaints. The recommended change to policy and procedure resulted in a decrease in customer complaints as well as an increase in staff satisfaction.

Design of the dispute resolution system: Once the need for a dispute resolution system has been identified, advocates can play an important role as part of the design team. In determining the purpose and goals of the system, advocates may provide specialized insight into the application of legal processes and contractual and legal obligations. Depending on their area of expertise and training, advocates may participate in designing a series of steps to deal with a specific class of issues and/or reviewing and approving the final product. Where specialized dispute resolution expertise is required, advocates may recommend a practitioner to consult or assist. In any event, the best dispute resolution design is developed with input from, and consideration of, all the stakeholders including counsel, staff, front-line managers, unions, contractors and possible clients.

Participation in the dispute resolution processes: Dispute resolution systems may use case management processes such as monitoring and tracking files, using time limits, and spotting audits, in addition to dispute resolution processes such as mediation, early neutral evaluation, med-arb and arbitration. The advocate may participate as part of the pre-screening process, as a participant advocating on behalf of a particular party, or as a third party intervenor. Functioning as counsel or a representative of a party may be integral to a particular advocate's role, and the need for legal advocacy during any given process should be reviewed. Corporate counsel or those counsel retained privately to represent organizations should consider carefully any participation in a third party neutral role. Any counsel intervening as fact-finder, mediator or facilitator should consider the potential apprehension of bias by the participants and the possibility of professional conflict of interest.

Defence of the dispute resolution system: Organizational policies, procedures and dispute resolution systems have come under the scrutiny of courts and tribunals. The typical issues include concerns about consistency of application to all parties, lack of clarity with regard to process, lack of fairness, due process, confidentiality, disclosure, and the timing of any action taken. For example, the disclosure requirements for claimants and the integrity of the sharing of information may impact an organization's ability to defend the outcome of an ad hoc ADR system addressing a particular class of claimants. When ADR systems are designed and implemented to assist in settling a class action, the process may come under the scrutiny of a judge in certification proceedings. In anticipation of such scrutiny, advocates should consider obtaining a written independent expert evaluation of their system by a bona fide ADR expert in the field. In *Tse v. Trow Consulting Engineers Ltd.*,[6] Cumming J. articulated a list of factors essential to having a policy accepted as effective by the courts:

(1) The rules must be distributed.
(2) The employees must know the rules.
(3) The rules must be consistently enforced.
(4) The employees must be warned that they will be terminated if a rule is breached.
(5) The rules must be reasonable.

These general rules may also apply to in-house dispute resolution systems.

In-house systems: With regard to the successful design and implementation of in-house dispute resolution systems, the role of both corporate and external counsel is again integral. Advocates may identify the need for a system or be called upon to defend it should the organization be challenged. Counsel may also recommend experienced dispute resolution practitioners to consult and assist. Advocates also have an important role in assisting organizations to manage conflict fairly and expeditiously the first time.

---

[6] (1995), 14 C.C.E.L. (2d) 132 (Ont. Ct. (Gen. Div.)).

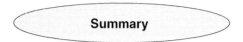

Summary

Institutionalized ADR processes need to take into consideration the suitability of a given process for a particular dispute. Training needs to be conducted so that staff are able to prescreen disputes and become effective participants in any interventions. Consideration must be given to the consent of the parties to any institutionalized process, as well as the terms and conditions of any intervention. Finally, any business organization should be concerned with evaluating outcomes and refining systems to meet organizational goals and objectives.

The optimal design of an ADR system should take into consideration compliance with organizational values, as was illustrated in the first case scenario on pp. 161*ff.* Contractual and statutory obligations also need to be considered in order to ensure that any ad hoc ADR program is not overruled by external obligations. There needs to be provided to the stakeholders education and guidance so that accessibility and full utilization of the system are ensured. Fair and open process should be used at all steps. Not all ADR processes are cost-effective, so any organization considering the design of an in-house ADR process needs to consider whether the systems can efficiently fulfil their mandate within budgetary constraints. Cost-effective screening of complaints as well as the swift resolution of minor complaints are all advantages of in-house ADR processes. Also of consideration are the terms of the interventions and the components of any final agreement. Lastly, organizations need to consider the initiation of fair and competent investigations where necessary.

APPENDIX 7.1
ADR SYSTEM DESIGN PRINCIPLES

☐   compliance with organizational values

☐   compliance with contractual and statutory obligations

☐   education and guidance for stakeholders

☐   use of a fair and open process

☐   efficient fulfilment of the mandate within budgetary constraints

☐   provision of adequate and cost-effective complaints screening

☐   swift resolution of "minor" complaints

☐   management of third party interventions and resolution

☐   initiation of fair and competent investigations where necessary

Appendix 7.2
Typical Program Goals/Objectives

- ☐ Reduction of costs, *e.g.*, settlement, legal, administrative costs
- ☐ reduced delay
- ☐ maintenance of, or improvement in, disputant satisfaction
- ☐ preservation of equity of outcomes
- ☐ promotion of a less contentious environment
- ☐ satisfaction of the organization's legal and cultural requirements

Appendix 7.3
In-House ADR Systems for Pre-Screening Cases

- ☐ Develop a system to refer targeted cases to ADR.
- ☐ Educate the stakeholders about appropriate alternatives.
- ☐ Pre-screen files to determine which types of dispute are suitable for ADR.
- ☐ Conduct the intake with the complainant to determine suitability.
- ☐ Seek the consent of all parties.
- ☐ Train the participants, staff, and managers to appropriate levels.
- ☐ Monitor, evaluate and modify the system.

Appendix 7.4
Terms of Intervention

- ☐ voluntary process/consent of the parties
- ☐ role of the mediator
- ☐ authority to settle
- ☐ process
    - ☐ joint session
    - ☐ individual meetings
    - ☐ shuttle diplomacy
    - ☐ telephone mediation
- ☐ commitment to fully participate
- ☐ confidentiality/without prejudice nature
- ☐ non-compellability of the mediator

APPENDIX 7.5
EVALUATION AND PROGRAM MODIFICATION

- ☐ Identify who will conduct the evaluation.
- ☐ Determine the terms of reference.
- ☐ Revisit the program goals.
- ☐ Develop appropriate measures of outcomes:
  - ☐ program outcomes
  - ☐ participant and case characteristics
  - ☐ program implementation characteristics
  - ☐ accountability to the profession and the public interest.
- ☐ Collect and analyze the data.

APPENDIX 7.6
INSTITUTIONALIZED ADR PROCEDURE

- ☐ suitability of disputes for ADR
- ☐ training
- ☐ consent of the parties
- ☐ terms and conditions of the intervention
- ☐ preparation
- ☐ evaluation of outcome

APPENDIX 7.7[7]
DISPUTE RESOLUTION PROCESS DESIGN

- ☐ diagnosis
  - ☐ data collection: consider
    - ☐ the current system
    - ☐ type and number of disputes
    - ☐ the parties to the disputes
    - ☐ baseline costs
  - ☐ needs analysis: identify the strengths and weaknesses of the existing system
  - ☐ conflict analysis
  - ☐ internal and external consultation
- ☐ design, which includes consideration of
  - ☐ the identification of program goals, which may include
    - ☐ reduced costs, *e.g.*, settlement, legal, administrative costs
    - ☐ delay reductions

---

[7] For a discussion of these points, see pp. 159-60.

      ☐ maintainenance of, or improvement in, disputant satisfaction
      ☐ equity of outcomes
      ☐ a less contentious environment

   ☐ participant and case characteristics: who the disputants are and how frequently disputes occur

   ☐ existing and desired program outcomes: are the existing organizational goals and mission statements directly relevant, and what are the causes of disputes

   ☐ existing transaction costs, satisfaction with outcomes, effect on relationships, and recurrence of disputes

   ☐ the current entry point to dispute resolution processes and other entry points which should be considered

   ☐ what dispute resolution options are available and/or desired

☐ implementation

   ☐ time frames and deadlines
   ☐ who will participate in the screening, convening and intervening
   ☐ education and training of internal and external participants
   ☐ the terms of interventions

☐ evaluation and program modification

   ☐ identifying who will conduct the evaluation and the terms of reference
   ☐ revisiting the program goals
   ☐ development of appropriate measures of outcomes
      ☐ program outcomes
      ☐ participant and case characteristics
      ☐ program implementation characteristics
   ☐ collection of data
   ☐ study of the design and the analysis plan

APPENDIX 7.8
ADR SCREENING TOOL AND CHECKLIST

This checklist is an example of an in-house ADR screening tool used by a major Canadian insurer. The individual criteria are more fully discussed on pp. 11-14.

☐ file type/category

☐ evidence/presence of fraudulent activity

☐ presence or absence of supporting documentation

☐ quantum requested

☐ presence of reserves in relation to the actual and anticipated costs of pursuing the file

☐ cost of the file: is the total cost within 25% of the total average, or has the file been identified as over limit

- ☐ length of time the file has been open
- ☐ current administrative and legal costs of the file
- ☐ anticipated administrative and legal costs of the file
- ☐ size of the group insurer and relationship with that client
- ☐ trends identified with a particular policyholder
- ☐ precedent value of the file

Conclusion

This book has endeavoured to provide advocates in the insurance industry with practical theory and knowledge to effectively represent their clients in various ADR processes. It has examined ADR definitions and choices, as well as strategic considerations when participating in the primary ADR processes: negotiation, mediation and arbitration. Checklists, case studies, and concrete examples of ADR clauses and systems have been provided to assist in selecting cases for ADR and tracking results.

Although once considered the flavour of the month, ADR is becoming less and less of an alternative, and more and more institutionalized, particularly in the insurance context. This can be seen by the use of court-mandated mediation in some jurisdictions and in insurance commissions such as those in Ontario and British Columbia. Law societies are now requiring lawyers to advise their clients as to the suitability of cases for ADR.

Studies have been done in Canada by the Insurance Commission of British Columbia, the National Canadian Bar Association Task Force, and the ADR Centre in Toronto to evaluate and refine the use of ADR. Not surprisingly, insurance companies have increasingly taken a systematic approach to in-house ADR, with processes in place to screen, convene and track the uses of ADR on a broad scale. In order to maximize effectiveness, insurance companies are approaching ADR systematically by:

- setting criteria to choose the appropriate type of dispute resolution;
- establishing guidelines to determine the appropriate entry point to ADR;
- establishing guidelines for choosing an intervenor;
- tracking internal and external costs;
- tracking results in order to fine-tune the ADR policies and guidelines;
- setting goals for mediation and preparing accordingly;
- establishing the expectations of the participants;

171

- upgrading negotiation skills to maximize effectiveness; and
- monitoring processes to identify trends and patterns.

This book has further set out how ADR advocates can prepare themselves and their clients for ADR. It has underscored the importance of selecting strategy and considering the individual strengths and weaknesses of one's own negotiating style in conjunction with the negotiating style of the opponent. Also reviewed were the benefits of using the client as part of the persuasion process, consideration of what documents are relevant and critical to obtaining the desired ADR outcome, and the need to be aware of the strategic choices in selecting an intervention, setting out the terms and conditions of the intervention, and selecting an intervenor.

ADR advocates should remember that the power of persuasion and the use of effective negotiation techniques are the cornerstone of most ADR processes. In the case of arbitration, many of the skills and techniques used in litigation will be applicable.

Advocates need to keep in mind their own underlying needs and interests, as well as those of their negotiating counterpart, when trying to further the position of their client.

Last, but not least, advocates have a role to play in setting the groundwork for ADR in terms of drafting dispute resolution clauses in policies, contracts and other kinds of insurance agreements, as well as participating in the design, implementation, evaluation and defence of any dispute resolution system put in place to resolve particular kinds of disputes.

The lessons learned from this book can be summarized as follows. Effective ADR advocates:

- understand the range of process choices available;
- recognize differences between private consensus processes and processes governed by recognized rules of procedure;
- recognize and work within ADR industry practice;
- recognize their own strengths and style preference;
- recognize the strengths and style preference of their counterparts;
- make strategic choices to create and claim value for their clients;
- recognize relationships and linkages between clients, advocates and organizations; and
- advance the interests of those they represent in a skilled, informed and professional manner.

Most importantly, effective advocates engage in continuous learning and re-evaluation of their techniques and knowledge in the face of an increasingly sophisticated ADR landscape. In the words of Mr. Justice Willard Estey (formerly of the Supreme Court of Canada), advocates should keep in mind that: "Unlike fine wine, disputes do not improve with age."

Index

Arbitration — *continued*

    conduct of hearing — *continued*

        summation and legal argument, 116

    generally, 111-12

    litigation vs. —

        factors, 21-2

        generally, 9-10

    pre-arbitration process, 113-14

    procedural matters. *See* conduct of hearing — procedural matters

    witnesses, 118-20

        conduct of, 118-19

        expert, 120

        preparation of, 119

        suggestions re, 119

Barriers to Settlement. *See* Settlement Barriers

Brief. *See* ADR Brief, Preparation of

Checklists

    ADR organizations, 28-9

    ADR screening criteria, 26-7, 169-70

    ADR system design —

        evaluation and program modification, 168

        in-house systems for pre-screening cases, 167

        institutionalized procedure, 168

        principles of, 166

        process design, 168-9

        program goals, 167

    agreement to mediate, components of, 95

    barriers to resolving cases, 27

    counsel and client preparation for ADR, 38-9

    dispute resolution clauses, 155

    drafting settlement documents, suggestions for, 40

    effective negotiation and mediation, 39

    implementing an ADR process, considerations in, 28

    legislation, Canadian arbitration, 120-21

    mandatory mediation, considerations when participating in, 99

    mediation brief, components of, 40

    negotiation —

        strategies/tactics, 62

        traps, 62

    strategic considerations for using mediation, 27

    terms of intervention, 167

    third party intervenor, considerations in choosing, 28